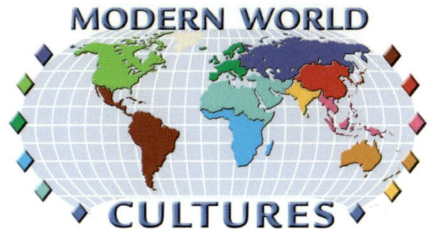

MODERN WORLD CULTURES

Africa South of the Sahara

◆

Australia and the Pacific

◆

East Asia

◆

Europe

◆

Latin America

◆

North Africa and the Middle East

◆

Northern America

◆

Russia and
the Former Soviet Republics

◆

South Asia

◆

Southeast Asia

◆

This is what the earth looks like at night. This image is actually a composite of hundreds of pictures made by orbiting satellites. Man-made lights highlight the developed or populated areas of the earth's surface. The dark areas include the central parts of South America, Africa, Asia, and Australia.

(Credit: C. Mayhew and R. Simmon; NASA/GSFC, NOAA/NGDC, DMSP Digital Archive.)

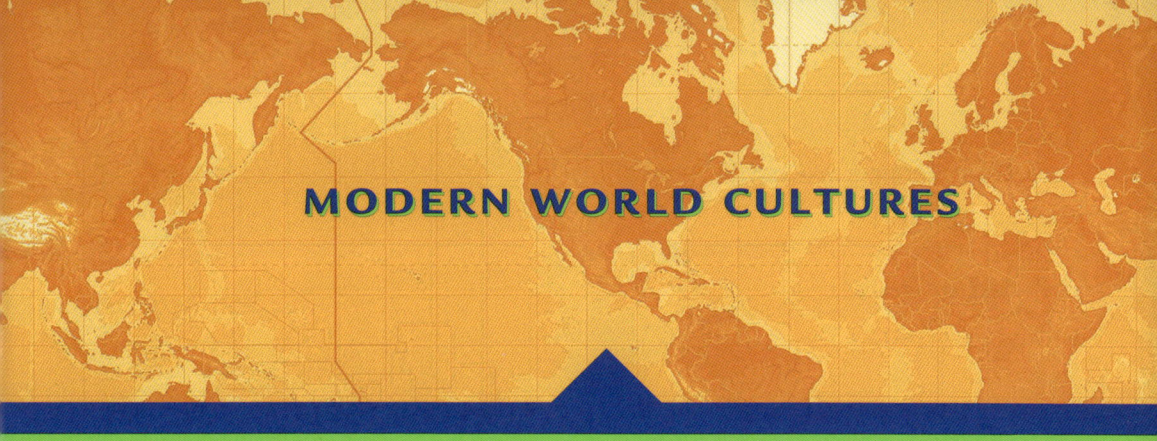

Northern America

Kristi L. Desaulniers and
Charles F. Gritzner

Series Consulting Editor
Charles F. Gritzner
South Dakota State University

An imprint of Infobase Publishing

Cover: Farmers rake hay in Vermont.

Northern America

Copyright © 2006 by Infobase Publishing

All rights reserved. No part of this book may be reproduced or utilized in any form or by any means, electronic or mechanical, including photocopying, recording, or by any information storage or retrieval systems, without permission in writing from the publisher. For information contact:

Chelsea House
An imprint of Infobase Publishing
132 West 31st Street
New York NY 10001

Library of Congress Cataloging-in-Publication Data

Desaulniers, Kristi L.
  Northern America / Kristi L. Desaulniers and Charles F. Gritzner.
    p. cm. — (Modern world cultures)
  Includes bibliographical references and index.
  ISBN 0-7910-8141-9 (hard cover)
  1. North America. 2. North America—Geography. I. Gritzner, Charles F. II. Title. III. Series.
  E38.D375 2005
  917—dc22
                                  2005031766

Chelsea House books are available at special discounts when purchased in bulk quantities for businesses, associations, institutions, or sales promotions. Please call our Special Sales Department in New York at (212) 967-8800 or (800) 322-8755.

You can find Chelsea House on the World Wide Web at http://www.chelseahouse.com

Text and cover design by Takeshi Takahashi

Printed in the United States of America

Bang MCC 10 9 8 7 6 5 4 3 2 1

This book is printed on acid-free paper.

All links and web addresses were checked and verified to be correct at the time of publication. Because of the dynamic nature of the web, some addresses and links may have changed since publication and may no longer be valid.

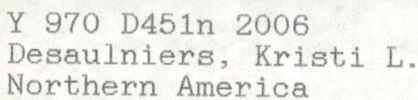

TABLE OF CONTENTS

	Introduction	vi
1	Northern America: A Region Blessed	1
2	Nature's Gifts and Challenges	10
3	Historical Geography	30
4	Population and Settlement	44
5	Culture and Society	63
6	Political Geography	73
7	Economic Geography	81
8	Regions of Northern America	94
9	Northern America Looks Ahead	104
	History at a Glance	111
	Further Reading	114
	Index	116

INTRODUCTION

Charles F. Gritzner

Geography is the key that unlocks the door to the world's wonders. There are, of course, many ways of viewing the world and its diverse physical and human features. In this series—MODERN WORLD CULTURES—the emphasis is on people and their cultures. As you step through the geographic door into the ten world cultures covered in this series, you will come to better know, understand, and appreciate the world's mosaic of peoples and how they live. You will see how different peoples adapt to, use, and change their natural environments. And you will be amazed at the vast differences in thinking, doing, and living practiced around the world. The MODERN WORLD CULTURES series was developed in response to many requests from librarians and teachers throughout the United States and Canada.

As you begin your reading tour of the world's major cultures, it is important that you understand three terms that are used throughout the series: geography, culture, and region. These words and their meanings are often misunderstood. **Geography** is an age-old way of viewing the varied features of Earth's surface. In fact, it is the oldest of the existing sciences! People have always had a need to know about and understand their surroundings. In times past, a people's world was their immediate surroundings; today, our world is global in scope. Events occuring half a world away can and often do have an immediate impact on our lives. If we, either individually or as a nation of peoples, are to be successful in the global community, it is essential that we know and understand our neighbors, regardless of who they are or where they may live.

Geography and history are similar in many ways; both are methodologies—distinct ways of viewing things and events. Historians are concerned with time, or when events happened. Geographers, on the other hand, are concerned with space, or where things are located. In essence, geographers ask: "What is where, why there, and why care?" in regard to various physical and human features of Earth's surface.

Culture has many definitions. For this series and for most geographers and anthropologists, it refers to a people's way of life. This means the totality of everything we possess because we are human, such as our ideas, beliefs, and customs, including language, religious beliefs, and all knowledge. Tools and skills also are an important aspect of culture. Different cultures, after all, have different types of technology and levels of technological attainment that they can use in performing various tasks. Finally, culture includes social interactions—the ways different people interact with one another individually and as groups.

Finally, the idea of **region** is one geographers use to organize and analyze geographic information spatially. A region is an area that is set apart from others on the basis of one or more unifying elements. Language, religion, and major types of economic activity are traits that often are used by geographers to separate one region from another. Most geographers, for example, see a cultural division between Northern, or Anglo, America and Latin America. That "line" is usually drawn at the U.S.-Mexico boundary, although there is a broad area of transition and no actual cultural line exists.

The ten culture regions presented in this series have been selected on the basis of their individuality, or uniqueness. As you tour the world's culture realms, you will learn something of their natural environment, history, and way of living. You will also learn about their population and settlement, how they govern themselves, and how they make their living. Finally, you will take a peek into the future in the hope of identifying each region's challenges and prospects. Enjoy your trip!

Charles F. "Fritz" Gritzner
Department of Geography
South Dakota State University
May 2005

CHAPTER 1

Northern America: A Region Blessed

The culture region of Northern America has been blessed in countless ways. It is blessed by nature: No area of comparable size in the world exhibits greater environmental diversity or abundance in terms of resource wealth. It has been blessed by history: Although no stranger to human strife, the region has been less ravaged by conflict than any area of comparable size in the world. It has been blessed culturally: Never in all of human history have more people of more varied cultural backgrounds joined and melded to form a relatively unified cultural "melting pot."

Northern America is unique among the world's cultural realms in many other ways. It is composed of only two countries, Canada and the United States. Although both countries have substantial minority populations, throughout the region the fundamental culture (way of life) is quite similar. In Canada, for example, people of French heritage take great pride in their cultural uniqueness, but the way they live on a day-to-day basis differs little from that of Anglo (English-speaking) Canadians.

Someone who travels between the United States and Canada will note few differences and feel little discomfort. To appreciate this relative homogeneity, one must have traveled in other culture realms. In the European culture region, for example, it is possible to travel through a half-dozen or more cultural microrealms, each with its own languages, diet, architectural style, and other observable traits, in a single day! In Northern America, one can travel from the remote shores of the Arctic Ocean to Miami, Florida, or Honolulu, Hawaii, and feel "at home" in a cultural sense.

CULTURE REGIONS

Culture is a word with many different meanings. For purposes of this book, it can be defined as learned (rather than biologically acquired) human behavior. What we learn determines the way we live. A culture is a human society that shares a common way of life. Most, if not all, members of the group share similar ideas, outlooks, values, institutions, technology, behaviors, and other aspects of life.

Regions can best be thought of as geographers' "convenience packages." They are areas that are in some way unique, or set apart, from others. A region must possess one or more similar elements (historians use centuries, periods, and eras in much the same way). In essence, the regional concept allows geographers to say, "this area is like this" and "that area is like that." The Northern American culture region, then, is an area in which most people share a somewhat similar way of life. The differences between the Western Hemisphere's two culture regions—Anglo (or Northern) America and Latin America—

Northern America: A Region Blessed

illustrate the point. Simply stated, people who live in Edmonton, Alberta, Canada, and Orlando, Florida, will have much more in common with one another than they will with residents of Mexico City or Lima, Peru.

At best, regions are abstractions that are often little more than stereotypical or "average" conditions. Throughout this book, the authors often write in very general and broadly sweeping terms. For every "rule," however, geographically there are often one or more "exceptions." This illustrates both a major strength and a primary weakness of the regional concept. Using the idea of regions allows the user to identify an area and speak of its primary characteristics in very general terms. In doing so, however, it tends to ignore conditions that do not conform to the generalization. Referring to "Anglo America," for example, ignores the French-speaking Canadians and other non-English-speaking peoples. Readers must recognize and understand this problem.

To the best of the authors' knowledge, this book represents the first use of the term *Northern America* in reference to this cultural realm. In the past, it has been almost universally recognized as *Anglo America*, based on the dominance of the English language and other British culture traits within the region. Clearly, however, this designation ignores the rich diversity of minority cultures that flourish within the region. These include Native American peoples of numerous cultures, French Canadians, the rapidly growing Hispanic and Asian communities, and others. To avoid such conflict, many scholars now use *North America*. The authors disagree with this emerging practice. Adopting a continental place name to designate a culture region is both confusing and misleading. Geographically, North America and South America are continents, whereas Anglo America and Latin America are culture regions. To avoid confusion and the appearance of cultural bias, the authors have elected to create and use a neutral term: *Northern America.*

4 Northern America

This is a general physical map of Northern America. The topography of the region varies, and two of the more prominent geographical features are the Great Plains and the Rocky Mountains.

Geographically, the Northern American culture region spans that part of the North American continent that lies north of the United States–Mexico border. With an area of slightly more than 7.6 million square miles (19.6 million square kilometers), it is exceeded in area only by Russia and the former Soviet republics. It is also the most diverse in terms of physical characteristics—its land and water features, climates and ecosystems, and natural resource wealth. With a population of approximately 330 million, however, only the culture region that comprises Australia, New Zealand, and the Pacific has fewer people, and only the former Soviet Union has a lower population density. Clearly, there is ample room and opportunity for both population and land use activities to expand within the region.

WHAT UNIFIES NORTHERN AMERICA?

By definition, all regions possess certain features or characteristics that set them apart from others. Identifying those traits can be a very formidable task, because any list of traits is subject to individual interpretation and selection. As you might imagine, many geographers, historians, and others have attempted to identify and explain the "unique character" or elements of unity that set Northern America apart from other culture regions. No two lists include the same characteristics. What follows is a list of elements that the authors believe contribute to Northern America's unique character.

1. **European Culture Was Transplanted to a New Land That Offered New Opportunities and Challenges**

Today, the dominant population and culture of Northern America is of European origin. Because the culture originated primarily in northwestern Europe, the primary language is English; the dominant religion is Protestantism (although Catholicism is strong as well); ideas of democracy, a free-market economy, and social equality are strong; and industry and urbanization are well developed. In this culture's new setting, many innovations occurred.

2. **Aboriginal (Native) Cultures Were Submerged by European Peoples and Their Way of Life**

Before the arrival of Europeans, the Americas were home to many varied native peoples. Throughout what is now Northern America, indigenous cultures have largely been replaced by the now-dominant European-introduced and often imposed way of living.

3. **An Abundance of Space and Natural Resources Lured Migrating Peoples**

It is safe to say that never before have migrating peoples invaded an area with more unoccupied (or underoccupied) high-quality land or land more richly endowed with abundant and varied natural resources. In terms of space, a seemingly endless expanse of potentially productive land stretched "from sea to shining sea." Because of this abundance, until recently, a frontier attitude toward the natural environment has existed. Little care or concern was given to the pollution of water and air, the destruction of forests and erosion of soil, or the waste of mineral resources.

4. **Huge Areas Remain Open to Human Settlement and Economic Development**

Much of the world appears to suffer from overpopulation, but Northern America offers a vast area of land suitable for settlement and development. The idea of new land and opportunity lying "just over the horizon" has been a key theme in the culture history of both Canada and the United States. Perhaps 2 million square miles (5.9 million square kilometers)—the central and western interior of the United States and much of Canada—can support millions of additional people with existing technologies and a comfortable living standard. Economic incentives must exist before this will occur.

5. **Cultural Assimilation Occurred on a Grand Scale**

What has happened culturally in the United States and much of Canada is unique in the human experience. The original national motto of the United States is *E pluribus unum*, a

Latin phrase that means "from many, one." With few exceptions, people from hundreds of different cultures have come together to form one Northern American way of life. Never before or since has such cultural assimilation occurred on such a grand scale. It is a process that continues today.

6. **Individuals Enjoy Great Personal Freedom and Protection Under the Law**

Perhaps more so than any other people in the world, Northern Americans are free, within the limits of the law and customs, to be themselves. They can express their thoughts, beliefs, and individuality. Canadians and Americans enjoy tremendous mobility—both vertically, on the so-called socioeconomic scale, and horizontally, in terms of migration, circulation, and information exchange.

7. **Northern America Is a Global Power**

Economically, militarily, materialistically, and as a center of innovations and ideas, Northern America is unsurpassed as a global powerhouse. Although Northern America (particularly the United States) is often criticized by much of the global community, migration data suggest that Northern America remains the dream, envy, and desired destination of millions of people throughout the world.

8. **The Region's Population Is Deeply Immersed in Popular Culture**

Perhaps two of every three people in the world continue to practice what geographers call *folk culture*, or very traditional, self-sufficient lifestyles. In a folk culture, the way of living changes little from year to year or even from generation to generation. In contrast, Northern America is the global leader in creating and living by the traits identified with popular (contemporary) culture. Progress, fad, change, growth, and specialization are buzzwords by which most Canadians and Americans live. Northern American popular culture—dress, entertainment (music, movies, television programs, literature, and so on), scientific achievements, medicine, technology, ideology, and much more—floods

8 Northern America

The Statue of Liberty float rolls down to Times Square in Macy's seventy-eighth annual Thanksgiving Day Parade in New York City on November 25, 2004.

the world, bringing joy to some and evoking bitter hostility from others.

As you will learn, a number of significant differences between the United States and Canada do exist. Such differences tend to be rather insignificant when considered in the context of a major culture region. Canada, for example, is bilingual, with both English and French as official languages. Nonetheless, both tongues are Western European. Each of the foregoing characteristics, as well as significant differences between the two countries that compose the Northern American culture realm, will be discussed in much greater detail elsewhere in this book.

After this brief introduction, your journey through Northern America will begin with a tour of its marvelous natural environment. You will see people at work, culturally adapting to, using, and changing the lands and ecosystems that they occupy. Your trip will follow the footsteps of the people and events responsible for shaping this land and its unique culture. You will stop to view its people, patterns of settlement, and basic culture traits—the things that stamp Northern Americans with their cultural individuality and as a unique people. To understand Northern America, one also must study its institutions, social patterns, government, and economic systems and activities. Your travels would not be complete without taking side trips into each of Northern America's many subregions. Each of these areas forms a small piece of the mosaic that, when completed, presents a composite picture of Northern America. Finally, as your journey comes to an end, you will peek over the horizon in hope of gaining a vision of the future of this culture realm that has been blessed in so many ways.

CHAPTER 2

Nature's Gifts and Challenges

Nature has blessed Northern America. Its abundant resources and environmental diversity is unsurpassed. Landform features are varied and often spectacular. Vast rolling plains with rich soils are homes to the world's largest area of productive agricultural land. Within the region, all of the world's climates and ecosystems can be found. These range from Hawaii's steaming wet tropics to the parched deserts of the Southwest. Frigid polar conditions span the northern latitudes of Canada and Alaska. Such environmental diversity affords unparalleled opportunity for various types of human land use, economic development, and settlement. Water resources are abundant and include shorelines that face three of the world's five oceans, the world's largest network of freshwater lakes, and many large and useful rivers. The world's greatest tidal range—a whopping 52.5 feet (16 meters)—occurs in Canada's Bay of Fundy. Plant and animal life is varied and plentiful, as is the wealth of fossil fuels, metals, and other useful minerals.

As you will learn in this chapter, nature also presents some challenges. Many natural hazards pose a risk to life and property. This chapter focuses on the natural environment and its importance to the people of Northern America.

CULTURE AND NATURE

Cultural ecology—the study of relationships between humans and the natural environments that they occupy—is one of geography's most fundamental and time-honored traditions. Some geographers once believed that nature strongly influenced or even determined the way in which people lived. They spoke of groups such as "rain-forest people" or "desert people" as if they were mere pawns of nature. Within each of Earth's ecosystems, however, great cultural diversity—different ways of living, thinking, and doing—exists. Within Northern America, for example, culture is similar from place to place, yet the region is home to all of Earth's landform types, climates, and ecosystems. If nature played the deciding role, each different region would be home to a distinct way of life. This simply is not the case. Whether you are reading this book in Fairbanks, Alaska; Phoenix, Arizona; or Hilo, Hawaii—or anyplace in between—your culture is nearly the same.

Today, when considering the culture-environment relationship, most geographers identify three key elements. First, they want to know how different cultures adapt to environmental conditions. Second, they study how various elements of the natural environment and its resources are used. Finally, they are interested in knowing how human activity has changed the environment and the human consequences of such changes. Each of these themes is considered, as appropriate, in the following discussion of the natural environment.

LAND FEATURES

Northern America's land features offer remarkable contrasts. Within the region, each major landform type—plains, hills, plateaus, and mountains—occurs over vast areas. Such diversity is important because each type of feature presents different options (or perhaps obstacles) for land use. Think for a moment of the type of landform environment best suited to each of the following activities: skiing (steep slopes), grain farming using large mechanized equipment (broad plains), building ground transportation linkages and large urban areas (relatively flat, stable land), shipping from a harbor (protected coastal indentation), building a dam and reservoir (deep, narrow valley), and attracting tourists (unusual or scenic natural feature). What activities can you think of for which each of those environments is poorly suited?

Northern America's major landforms are shared by the United States and Canada. On a map of the region's terrain, three major patterns appear: coastal lowlands backed by highlands in the east and Gulf Coast; vast low-lying plains in the interior, stretching from the Gulf of Mexico to Hudson Bay and the Arctic Ocean; and of rugged mountains, plateaus, and basins in the west.

Atlantic and Gulf Coastal Plains

The east coast is bordered by a low, gently rolling coastal plain that extends from Texas to the Gulf of St. Lawrence. The lowlands that border the Gulf of Mexico form the Gulf coastal plain. Those that border the ocean from eastern Florida northward into Canada form the Atlantic coastal plain. These plains are areas of generally fertile soil that support a high population density. Ground transportation linkages, from earliest European settlement, were easy and relatively inexpensive to build. Coastal indentations and islands have provided places of shelter for seaports around which many urban centers grew. Tampa, Florida; New York City; Boston, Massachusetts; and

Halifax, Nova Scotia, all thrived because of their location on natural harbors.

Inland from the coastal plains, land rises abruptly to form the Piedmont, a hilly upland that lies at the eastern foot of the Appalachian Mountains. Where the Piedmont meets the coastal plain is a narrow zone called the *fall line*. The sharp break in terrain results in falls or rapids, which, in turn, form the head of navigation on streams that flow to the Atlantic. Here, goods being transported by water had to be transferred to land-based conveyances or vice versa. The rapid stream flow also could be harnessed to power water mills. To take advantage of these natural opportunities, many communities were established along the fall line. Columbia, South Carolina; Raleigh, North Carolina; Richmond, Virginia; and Lowell, Massachusetts, are among the cities that benefited from this unique natural condition.

Appalachian Mountains

To the west of the Piedmont lie the Appalachian Mountains and associated features. These ancient folded mountains with softly rounded crests extend from Alabama northward into eastern Canada. They reach their highest elevation atop North Carolina's Mount Mitchell (6,684 feet; 2,037 meters). Viewed from above, they form a generally southwest-to-northeast-trending series of parallel ridges and valleys. The mountains form a natural barrier between the coastal plain and interior of the continent. In places, ancient rivers carved out narrow east–west-trending valleys as the mountains gradually rose millions of years ago. These valleys, called *gaps*, created openings that are easily followed by trails, highways, and railroads. Because of the ruggedness of terrain, much of Appalachia remained relatively isolated for years. Isolation allowed the scattered and fiercely independent people of this region to retain traditional ways of living long after most Northern Americans had adopted a fast-paced and rapidly changing popular culture.

St. Lawrence–Great Lakes Lowlands and Canadian Shield

In Canada, to the west of the Appalachians, lie two regions that do not extend into the United States. Lowlands border the St. Lawrence River and also the Canadian side of the Great Lakes. Both features were formed during the Ice Age, when glaciers scoured basins and leveled terrain. When the glaciers began to melt and recede about 12,000 years ago, basins—including the Great Lakes—began to fill with water. Glacial meltwater also rushed down the St. Lawrence Valley, forming the river that now occupies the trench.

The Canadian shield is a horseshoe-shaped area of rolling uplands that covers nearly half of Canada. It is composed of very ancient rock that has been heavily worn down by millions of years of glacial erosion. The shield is an area of poor, thin soils and millions of lakes, wetlands, and small streams—all the result of the region's glacial past. At several sites, rivers that flow over falls or rapids have been harnessed to produce hydroelectric power. The shield also is rich in minerals, and mining accounts for much of the area's scant settlement and population. Because of the many lakes and rivers, few transportation routes penetrate the shield. Other than the far north, it is Northern America's least-populated area.

Interior Lowland Plains

In the central interior of Northern America is a vast lowland plain that extends from the Appalachians westward to the Rocky Mountains. The plains are divided into three regional divisions. The wetter eastern portion in the United States is called the Central Plains; the drier and slightly higher western portion is called the Great Plains; the northward extension of these into Canada is known as the Western Interior Plains. Most of the region has very good soil and ample moisture that help make it the world's largest and most productive grain-growing "breadbasket." It is also an area of extensive livestock grazing.

Nature's Gifts and Challenges

Rocky Mountains and Interior Basins and Plateaus

Much of the western interior of Northern America is a land of towering mountains, sprawling plateaus, and gaping canyons. It is a region of rugged, spectacular scenery. To a person traveling westward across the plains, the Rocky Mountains appear as a giant dark curtain on the distant horizon. Their majestic glaciated peaks offer some of Northern America's most impressive scenery. Colorado alone has 17 peaks that reach an elevation of more than 14,000 feet (4,267 meters). Although the Canadian Rockies are not as lofty, they are even more spectacular because of the jagged peaks formed by extensive glaciation. The Rockies actually are a series of ranges, each with a regional name, such as Sangre de Cristo in New Mexico and Colorado, Bitterroot in Montana and Idaho, Columbia in Canada, and Brooks in Alaska.

Lands to the west of the Rocky Mountains include three huge plateaus and a large stretch of relatively low, isolated mountains separated by broad basins. The Colorado Plateau is centered on the "Four Corners" area, where Arizona, New Mexico, Utah, and Colorado meet. It is a rugged area of spectacular cliffs, arches, gorges (including the Grand Canyon on the Colorado River in Arizona), and other erosional features. To the north, the volcanic Columbia Plateau covers portions of eastern Washington and Oregon and reaches into southern Idaho. In addition to many unique volcanic features, it offers a variety of spectacular erosional features, including Hell's Canyon on the Snake River and the "scablands" of eastern Washington. Scablands—bare rock with most soil removed—were created during the late Ice Age. A glacial lobe created an ice dam on the Clark Fork River near Sandpoint, Idaho, creating a huge inland water body, ancient Lake Missoula. When the lake reached a depth of perhaps 2,000 feet (610 meters), the ice began to float. The resulting torrent of water—a volume estimated to have been ten times as great as the combined flow of all the world's rivers!—rushed toward the distant Pacific at

Northern America

This is a view of the Grand Canyon from Hopi Point, Arizona. Every year, over 5 million tourists visit the canyon. The canyon is 275 miles (443 kilometers) long and up to 1 mile (1,700 meters) deep.

speeds of up to 65 miles per hour (105 kilometers per hour). The force of this vast flood removed or altered everything in its path and left an erosional landscape found nowhere else in the world. In the interior of Canada's British Columbia, the Fraser Plateau is a rugged and remote area of sparse settlement and few people.

Elsewhere in the region, stretching from west Texas to the Pacific Coast of western Alaska, the terrain is dotted with scattered mountain ranges that are separated by broad basins. Many of the basins have no drainage outlet. Salts deposited in the basins by inflowing water cannot be removed. The result is an accumulation of salts such as the deep deposits of Utah's Bonneville Salt Flats and saline water bodies such as Great Salt Lake and Southern California's Salton Sea.

Nature's Gifts and Challenges

In the interior West, rugged terrain and a lack of moisture combine to make most types of land use—including building transportation linkages—somewhat difficult and costly. Much of the region has undergone two stages of settlement: Until the mid-1900s, many locations experienced a "boom and bust" economy based on mining. During recent decades, a spurt in development has been fueled primarily by increased tourism and people moving to the region because of its weather, scenery, and other natural amenities.

Pacific Coast Mountains and Valleys

The Pacific Coast, which extends from California to Alaska and includes Hawaii, is a region of mountains and scattered large, fertile valleys. In the United States, low coastal ranges border the Pacific. In many places, including San Diego and San Francisco, California; Seattle, Washington; Vancouver, British Columbia; and Anchorage, Alaska, large natural indentations form protected harbors. Inland from the coast are areas of very productive farmlands, including California's Imperial and Central valleys and the Willamette Valley in Oregon.

Farther inland lie mountain ranges that geologically are part of a continuous range that surrounds nearly all of the Pacific Ocean basin. The Sierra Nevada range forms the huge "backbone" of central California. Here, Mount Whitney, the highest peak in the adjoining 48 states, reaches an elevation of 14,494 feet (4,418 meters). Just 70 miles (113 kilometers) to the east, Death Valley plunges to a depth of 282 feet (86 meters) below sea level, the lowest area of dry land in the Western Hemisphere.

Beginning in northern California and extending northward into Washington are the Cascades, a volcanic range. The highest peak is majestic snowcapped Mount Rainier, which towers 14,410 feet (4,392 meters) above the surrounding lowlands. In Canada and Alaska, higher mountains hug the coast, creating spectacular scenery. Here, the Coast Ranges form an almost continuous barrier of offshore islands, leaving a semiprotected "inland" water passage. The coast is broken with deep fjords, glacially scoured trenches that are now arms of the sea. Inland, Canada's Mount Logan reaches an elevation of 19,550 feet (5,959 meters) and Alaska's snow- and glacier-shrouded Mount McKinley, also called Denali, soars to 20,320 feet (6,194 meters), the highest peak in North America.

The Hawaiian Islands were formed by volcanic activity, a process that continues to occur regularly on the big island of Hawaii. Despite their tropical location, the volcanic peaks of Mauna Kea and Mauna Loa occasionally sport crowns of snow. Mauna Kea rises 20,000 feet (6,096 meters) from the floor of the Pacific and reaches an elevation of 13,796 feet (4,205 meters). With a bottom-to-top span of almost 34,000 feet (10,360 meters), it is the world's "tallest" mountain!

CLIMATES AND ECOSYSTEMS

Most of Northern America lies within the middle latitudes. Only in the far north does it extend into the bitterly cold polar latitudes, and only the Hawaiian Islands fall within the tropical zone. The region's position is of considerable geographical importance. Areas that experience extreme climatic conditions (cold, dry, hot, wet, or a combination of these) can be much more difficult and costly to develop. As a result, they may attract fewer people. The middle latitudes, however, tend to experience more moderate weather (day-to-day conditions) and climate (average weather over decades). They therefore tend to be easier to develop. Historically, they also were more attractive to other mid-latitude peoples seeking new lands. The cultural importance of this reality will be discussed in greater depth in later chapters.

Northern America is unique in that it is the world's only culture realm that includes each of the world's climates and ecosystems somewhere within its territory. This unmatched variety of environmental conditions is important for several

Nature's Gifts and Challenges 19

Northern America stretches south almost to the Tropic of Cancer and north to the Arctic Circle, and includes a vast array of climates.

reasons. First, climate is the primary influence on ecosystems. The great variety of conditions contributes to a tremendous diversity of flora and fauna (plants and animals), soil types, and moisture conditions. Second, all human activities, including the growing of any type of agricultural crop, can find a suitable environmental "home" someplace within the region. Finally, "variety," it has been said, "is the spice of life." Geographically, people enjoy and seem to thrive in environments that offer a variety of conditions and opportunities.

Most of eastern Northern America experiences a humid continental climate. Depending on latitude, winters are cool in the south and cold in the north and summers are hot in the south and cool in the north. The entire region receives ample rainfall to support agricultural crops or dense vegetation, and moisture is distributed fairly evenly throughout the year. Under natural conditions, the region would support a dense cover of needleleaf evergreen, broadleaf deciduous, or mixed forests. Today, much of the natural vegetation cover has been removed for settlements, agriculture, and other types of human land use. In the southern United States, however, much of the land that was once forest covered and then farmed is again reverting to woodland.

In the central interior of Northern America, the climate is considerably drier and temperature extremes are greater. Most of the area receives 10 to 20 inches (25 to 50 centimeters) of precipitation annually, much of which falls in summer thundershowers. Temperatures range from hot to frigid, depending on latitude and season. Before the arrival of European settlers, much of the central interior was covered with a sea of grass. Tall prairie grasses dominated the landscape of the wetter eastern margin, and shorter steppe grasslands thrived in the drier western edge. This was home to the American bison (buffalo), millions of which roamed the grass-covered plains. Today, cultivated grains have largely replaced the natural grasslands and domesticated livestock herds have replaced the native bison.

Nature's Gifts and Challenges 21

In the 1800s, the bison population seemed limitless, and few laws protected the animals. They were hunted by men like "Buffalo Bill" Cody for their meat, by traders for their valuable hides, and by settlers to make room for cattle. From 1872 to 1874 alone, over three million were killed. Today, about 120,000 survive.

Between the eastern slopes of the Sierra Nevada, Cascades, and Canadian Pacific ranges and the Rockies, the climate is dry and temperatures vary greatly depending on latitude, elevation, and, of course, season. The region's aridity results from the high western mountains blocking moisture-bearing winds from the Pacific. East of the Pacific ranges, only scattered high mountains receive enough moisture to support forest growth. Throughout most of the region, annual average precipitation measures less than 10 inches (25 centimeters), reaching a low on the parched desert floor of Death Valley, which receives less than 1.5 inches (3.8 centimeters) per year. Temperatures have reached a sizzling 135°F (57°C) in California's Death Valley. Ironically, during the very wet spring of 2005, much of Death

Valley's floor became a huge lake. Throughout the region, nearly all locations experience cool to cold winter temperatures.

Coastal Southern California experiences a mild Mediterranean climate. It lacks temperature extremes and, despite a prolonged summer drought, has enough moisture to support fairly lush vegetation cover. From Northern California northward to Alaska, heavy coastal rainfall supports a dense cover of needleleaf evergreen forests. Until recent years, these forests provided much of Northern America's high-quality construction wood harvest.

Hawaii, although tropical, supports a variety of microclimatic conditions and ecosystems. On the island of Kauai, one can stand in an area of short grasses, scattered cacti, and less than 10 inches (25 centimeters) of annual rainfall and gaze on the world's wettest spot—Mount Waialeale (annual average 460 inches [1,168 centimeters] of rainfall)—only a few miles away!

The far north is a region of short summers and very long harsh winters. Moisture is scant, but evaporation is low. A broad band of taiga (also called "boreal forest") extends from interior Alaska to the shores of the Atlantic Ocean north of the St. Lawrence River. This dense forest of spruce, larch, pine, and aspen is the largest in North America. Because of its remote location and the scrawny size of most trees, however, only recently has logging begun here. The forests teem with wildlife, including deer, elk, moose, and bears. North of the taiga is the tundra, a region of mosses, lichens, grasses, and small flowering plants. Here, the growing season is too short and the soil too shallow for trees to grow. This fragile land is home to large herds of caribou and other wildlife.

WATER FEATURES

Water is essential to life. In areas that have an abundance of moisture, population density tends to be high and, under natural conditions, vegetation is plentiful. Where moisture is scarce, population thins out and vegetation becomes scant.

Generally speaking, it can be said that the eastern half of Northern America has ample water resources, including lakes, rivers, and groundwater. In many places, however, it faces problems of pollution and overuse. Much of the western half of the region lacks adequate water resources.

Lakes

An estimated 90 percent of the world's lakes occupy basins scoured by glaciers. During the Ice Age, nearly all of Canada and most of the United States north of the Missouri and Ohio rivers was covered by continental ice sheets. A detailed map of any part of the United States or Canada that was glaciated will reveal thousands of lakes. Outside the glaciated areas, very few natural lakes (as opposed to reservoirs, or lakes located behind dams) exist.

The Great Lakes, shared by the United States and Canada, form the world's largest body of freshwater. Their natural outflow is through the St. Lawrence River. Since 1959, ships have been able to navigate all of the lakes and sail into the Atlantic Ocean through the St. Lawrence Seaway. Ocean-going ships can leave the most inland port city, Duluth, Minnesota, located at the western tip of Lake Superior, and eventually reach the Atlantic, 2,340 miles (3,766 kilometers) distant. On its trip, a ship would pass through four of the five Great Lakes and descend more than 600 feet (183 meters) through a network of 19 locks and 6 canals.

Rivers

Northern America is drained by a number of great rivers. The largest system is that formed by the Missouri, Ohio, and Mississippi rivers and their many tributaries. Combined, they drain an area of about 1,245,000 square miles (3,225,000 square kilometers), an area surpassed only by South America's Amazon and Africa's Congo rivers.

From the eastern slope of the Rocky Mountains in Montana, the combined Missouri–Mississippi River system flows 3,700 miles (5,970 kilometers). It finally reaches the Gulf of

Northern America

The Soo Locks in Sault Sainte Marie, Michigan, are an indispensable gateway along the Great Lakes shipping route. Vessels pass through the locks more than 7,000 times annually.

Mexico through its bird's-foot-shaped delta south of New Orleans, Louisiana. Barges can travel upstream on the Missouri River to Sioux City, Iowa; the Ohio River to Pittsburgh, Pennsylvania; and the Mississippi to St. Paul, Minnesota.

In the Southwest, the Colorado River and Rio Grande cascade southward from the Colorado Rockies. Although relatively small in volume, these rivers create oases in otherwise arid areas. As a result, they have attracted considerable human settlement, much of which is based on irrigated agriculture. The importance of water in a desert is illustrated by the Colorado River. Between the point where it enters the state of Arizona and its mouth in the Gulf of California, the river's flow is controlled by eight dams and reservoirs, including Glen Canyon Dam and Lake Powell on the Utah–Arizona border, and the huge Hoover Dam and Lake Mead just east of Las Vegas, Nevada. So much of the river's flow is diverted for human, industrial, and agricultural use in Arizona, California, Nevada, and Mexico that almost no water reaches its delta at the head of the Gulf of California. In addition, hydroelectric power is produced and the river and reservoirs provide wonderful recreational opportunities in an otherwise parched landscape.

Other important rivers in the United States include the Columbia in the Pacific Northwest and the Hudson River in the Northeast. Inland, the Tennessee River and its many tributaries were the focus of one of the nation's greatest reclamation projects, the Tennessee Valley Authority (TVA). Begun on the heels of the Great Depression of the 1930s, the TVA was one of the most ambitious engineering projects ever attempted. Dams were built to control flooding and produce hydroelectric energy. Canals were dug and locks were built to facilitate navigation. These and other related projects began to transform the previously impoverished region in many positive ways.

Canada's most important river, historically, economically, and in terms of human settlement, is the St. Lawrence. To the north, Alaska's Yukon River and Canada's Mackenzie River drain areas of very low population and little economic activity. Because of the sharp seasonal variability of their flow (up to 90 percent of their annual volumetric flow occurs in a two-month period after the spring thaw), the rivers cannot be harnessed for hydroelectric development and are of little use for navigation.

Human Use of Water Resources

Today, as in the past, water is a magnet for settlement, economic development, and transportation. Nearly all early settlements, whether native or European, bordered rivers, freshwater lakes, springs, or natural harbors. Water was used for domestic purposes, industry, and agriculture. It also served as a thoroughfare for easy travel before the days of railroads and highways. Mills for sawing timber or milling grain could be built at points where streams cascaded over falls or rapids. Fish provided a reliable source of food. The importance of water to settlement is often indicated in place names that include words such as "Lake," "River," "Port," "Harbor," "Springs," "Falls," and "Rapids." In arid regions, oasis sites often grew into thriving communities. Along coasts, settlements often were founded at or near the mouth of a navigable river or on a natural harbor.

Today, water resources are still of great importance. In addition to their historical uses, streams are now harnessed to provide electrical energy. In arid regions, water is transferred great distances, as is the case with diversion from the Colorado River to Phoenix and Tucson, Arizona, and the Los Angeles basin in southern California. California also diverts water from the Sierra Nevada southward to its major population centers. California is the most populated political unit in Northern America, with more than 35 million residents. Without the massive diversion of precious water resources, the state could support only a small fraction of its current population.

ENVIRONMENTAL HAZARDS

Although Northern America has been blessed by nature in countless ways, the region also has been cursed. No other region of comparable size is subject to a greater array of devastating natural hazards. From within the earth come shattering earthquakes and violent volcanic eruptions. From the atmosphere come torrential rains, pounding hail, freezing ice, and howling blizzards of snow or dust. Each year, nature's most violent storms, tornadoes and hurricanes, take a tragic toll on human life and property unfortunate enough to lie in their path. Waters, too, can pose an omnipresent hazard to humans and property. Few places are free of occasional drought, periodic river or lowland flooding, or coastal inundation by tsunamis (incorrectly called "tidal waves") or storm-driven waves. Rock

Nature's Gifts and Challenges 27

In terms of loss of life, the Galveston, Texas, hurricane of 1900 was the worst disaster in American history. More than 8,000 people perished September 8, 1900, when the Category 4 hurricane barreled into Galveston, where many people were on vacation. (The practice of naming hurricanes did not begin until 1953.)

and snow avalanches, mud flows, and other hazards caused by gravity often devastate property and people who live below.

Of course, not all places are subject to the ravages of all of the environmental hazards. In fact, natural hazards show a rather distinct pattern of regional distribution. Hurricanes, for example, wreak their havoc along the Gulf and Atlantic coasts. Downgraded to tropical storms, they often penetrate well into the interior, where they can cause devastating floods. In September 1900, a violent storm swept ashore from the Gulf of Mexico in the area of Galveston, Texas. Its fierce winds drove a wall of water across low-lying Galveston Island. By the time the howling winds and churning floodwaters receded, an estimated

8,000 people had died. As measured by loss of life, the Galveston hurricane ranks as Northern America's greatest natural disaster.

In late August 2005, Hurricane Katrina struck the Gulf Coast of Louisiana, Mississippi, and Alabama with powerful 145 mile-per-hour (235 kilometer-per-hour) winds. In her wake, Katrina left an estimated 1,200 deaths, 1.5 million people displaced, an area of 90,000 square miles (235,000 square kilometers) almost totally destroyed, and more than 200 billion dollars in property damage. In terms of destruction and cost, it was the greatest natural disaster in Northern American history. Because they require heat, hurricanes—tropical storms with winds in excess of 74 miles per hour (119 kilometers per hour)—occur during the summer and early autumn months.

Tornadoes, or "twisters," as they are often called, have occurred in most states and provinces but are concentrated in the continental interior. "Tornado Alley"—the path along which the greatest number of these treacherous storms occurs—is a belt several hundred miles wide that extends from Texas to the Great Lakes. These storms, with upward spiraling winds that can exceed 250 miles per hour (400 kilometers per hour), can destroy nearly everything in their path.

Earthquakes tend to be localized but can cause tremendous loss of life and property. Although the Pacific Coast—which lies on the Pacific Ring of Fire—is the most earthquake-prone area, seismic events have occurred in most areas of Northern America. San Francisco, located astride the well-known San Andreas Fault, is in constant peril, as is the Los Angeles area. In terms of loss of life, the 1906 San Francisco earthquake, with 500 deaths, remains the most tragic. Perhaps the most intense earthquake on record, which measured 9.2 on the Richter scale, by which earthquake intensity is measured, struck a huge area of southern Alaska in 1964. Although only 131 people lost their lives, much of the state's largest city, Anchorage, and several other communities lay in ruin.

Certainly one of the most spectacular events in Northern America's recent history was the violent 1980 eruption of Washington's Mount St. Helens. Fortunately, the peak is quite isolated and there was ample advance warning. A huge area was affected by the explosion and following nine-hour eruption. Fortunately, only 57 people died and property losses were minimal despite the incredible violence of the event.

Natural Disasters or Human Risk?

Cultural geographers question whether "natural" disasters actually exist. Nearly all hazards, after all, can be predicted. If you live on the Gulf or Atlantic coast, you *know* that a hurricane will eventually strike. The same holds true for people who live near fault zones on the West Coast, people who build homes in areas of highly combustible woodland, or those who live at the base of an active volcano such as Mount St. Helens.

Many hazard zones have highly desirable qualities. People are drawn to coastal waters, the shores of rivers and lakes, densely forested mountains, and other hazard zones. In so doing, they are taking a calculated risk: It won't happen to *me*.

Some places, of course, are much safer than others. Nearly all of Canada is relatively free of severely damaging events. In the United States, the northern Great Plains region is relatively hazard free. Ironically, a comparison of population patterns and property values clearly shows that the most hazardous areas also are those that are experiencing the greatest gains in population and increases in property value. Relatively safe areas such as the continental interior tend to be experiencing out-migration and stable or declining property values.

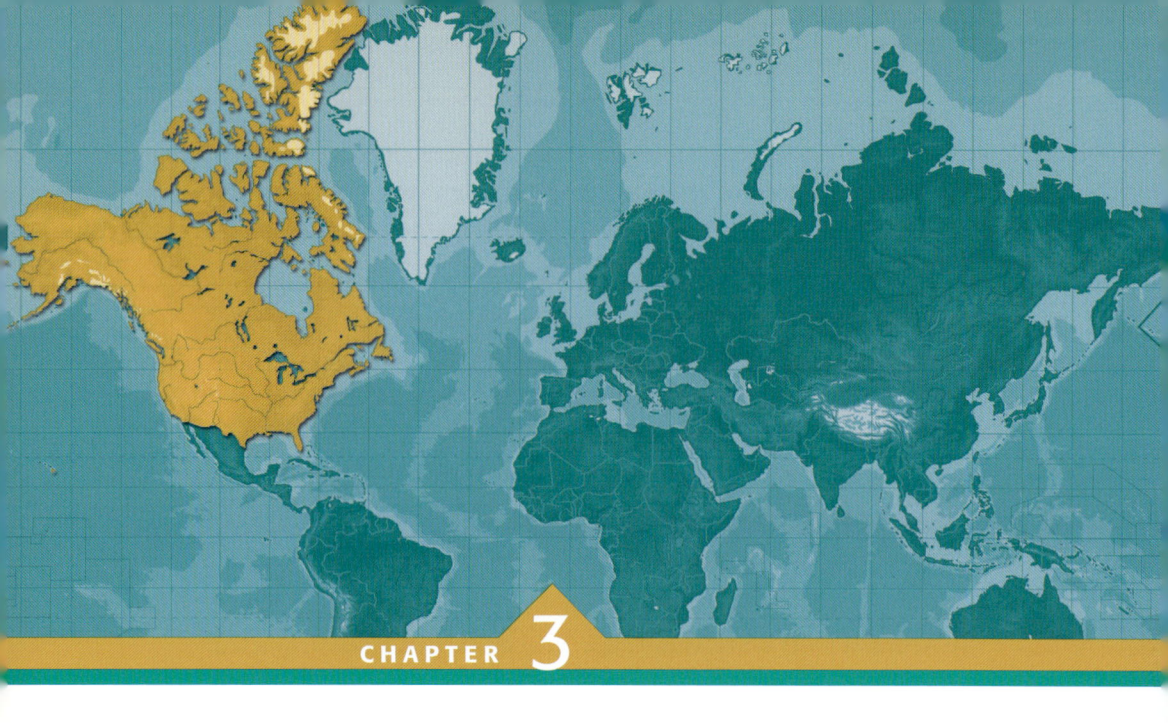

Historical Geography

Think for a moment about a person your age living in a distant land. How would your lives be similar? How would your lives be different? How might such similarities and differences be explained?

Throughout the world, people share certain similarities in the ways they live. Differences based on where people live do exist, yet there are common threads that define their culture, or way of life. For example, people have holidays and special occasions during which particular foods are enjoyed. They have belief systems, languages, ways of earning a living, forms of entertainment, and a heritage—all of which are unique to that particular region. *Why* certain traits or traditions have developed can be better investigated by studying a region's historical geography, with emphasis on its cultural history.

As you read in Chapter 2, Canada and the United States share many physical geographic features. In this chapter, you will explore the ways in which Northern America's culture history evolved. You will find that, in many ways, the United States and Canada share a common history, yet in other ways, they differ in terms of their past. Similar historical threads include pre-European native cultures; European exploration, settlement, and colonization; population growth as a result of immigration; westward expansion; and a wealth of natural resources.

THE FIRST AMERICANS

Northern America's first people came from elsewhere. Half a century ago, scientists believed that they knew who these early people were, where they came from, how and by what route they traveled to this new land, and when they arrived. Asian peoples, they believed, pursued large game animals across Beringia, the Bering Strait "land bridge"—exposed when the sea level dropped during the Ice Age. They then passed through an ice-free corridor located between two huge masses of glacial ice that covered much of northern North America. Finally, as suggested by the Clovis site and its unique stone projectile points, they reached what is now New Mexico perhaps 12,000 to 13,000 years ago.

Today, many scientists are less sure of this scenario. In fact, the origin of the first Americans appears to be a great unanswered "mystery." Archaeological finds have been interpreted by at least some scientists to suggest multiple origins of America's earliest people. Southeast Asia, Japan, and eastern Siberia have all been suggested as the source area(s), but so have Australia, Europe, and Africa. Some archaeologists still believe that the original theory holds true. A growing number of scientists now believe that this route would have been far too cold and inhospitable for travel, however, and some even doubt the existence of the proposed ice-free corridor.

Support for a coastal route is gaining. During the Ice Age, sea level was several hundred feet lower than it is now, and land that is now underwater would have been exposed—a natural corridor for human migration. Certain scientists even believe that some of the earliest settlers may have traveled by boat during at least part of their long journey. The time of arrival also is now in serious doubt. Various estimates based on the interpretation of "evidence" by scientists place the earliest arrivals at any time from perhaps 13,000 to more than 100,000 years ago!

Perhaps the full story of the earliest Northern Americans will never be known. In fact, the question is much more academic than practical in nature. Almost certainly, pre-European arrivals represented a variety of human physical types, including Mongoloid, Negroid, and Caucasoid. This suggests multiple migrations from different source areas, which almost certainly was the case. Such migrations may have occurred by both land and water over thousands of years.

NATIVE CULTURES

Native people of Northern America recognized themselves by many names, both as individual (tribal) groups and collectively. *Indian* is the most common term used in reference to them, but many prefer to be called "Native Americans," "First Americans," or "First Nations" ("First Nations" is preferred in Canada). *Indian*, after all, is derived from one of the great geographical errors of all time—Columbus's belief that he had reached the Indies of southeastern Asia.

Several things can be said with some certainty about the earliest Northern Americans. When Europeans arrived on the shores of the "New World," they reached a land that had been "discovered" and settled thousands of years earlier. The native peoples were dominantly East Asian in terms of physical characteristics and geographical origin. The ways of life practiced by native peoples varied greatly in terms of language, economic

The Anasazi cliff dwelling ruins in Mesa Verde, Colorado, are the best preserved ancient cliff dwellings in the United States. The name Anasazi is from the Navajo language and means "ancient ones."

activity, housing, dress, and many other aspects of culture. Levels of cultural attainment ranged from well-organized high level "civilizations" to small groups of isolated peoples who possessed a very meager level of material culture.

In the southwestern United States, Pueblo tribes grew crops of maize (corn), beans, and squash. Some, such as the Hohokam (in what is today central Arizona), practiced a very advanced type of irrigation, diverting water great distances in well-constructed canals. Many of their adobe (clay and straw) or stone structures remain today, a tribute to their building skills.

East of the Mississippi River and south of the Great Lakes and St. Lawrence River, woodland peoples practiced productive farming combined with hunting and fishing. An adequate and reliable food supply made relatively large populations, settled communities, and high levels of social organization possible.

Along the Pacific Coast from northern California through the Alaskan panhandle, many people turned to rivers and the sea for their livelihood. Here, salmon and other types of marine life provided an abundance of food. People were able to live in large, well-built wooden buildings in permanently settled communities. They also were skilled in the construction and use of sturdy watercraft.

Bison (buffalo) hunters occupied the continent's interior from the Rio Grande northward into central Canada. Millions of these huge beasts roamed the interior plains. They provided meat, hides, bone, horn, and sinew (thread), all of which were important resources to these skilled hunters. Because the bison were migratory, the Plains Indians were as well. As a result, they had few material possessions, often little more than their clothing, tools, and weapons.

In parts of the dry interior west, low populations of seasonally wandering peoples depended on hunting and gathering of wild seeds. Their material culture was the most meager of all Northern American peoples.

Across the vast subarctic region of taiga forest, people depended on caribou hunting, fishing, and gathering for their livelihood. Some groups made sturdy canoes from the bark of birch trees. During the winter, snowshoes and toboggans were used to make travel across the snow-covered surface easier. Their meager way of life stood in sharp contrast to that of the tundra and Arctic coast Inuit (Eskimo). Inuit material culture ranked among the most advanced of all the world's preagricultural peoples. It featured sturdy buildings, including the igloo. Travel was by dogsled in the winter and sleek kayaks and larger seagoing umiaks during the summer. As skilled hunters and fishermen, they had few equals. The Inuit harpoon is one of the most effective hunting weapons ever devised. Inuit clothing, designed to protect against temperatures that drop far below freezing for months at a time, is excellent. In fact, much of our own winter clothing design—jackets, gloves, headgear, and footwear—was adopted from the Inuit.

Northern America's native peoples made numerous contributions to present-day culture. Many land features are identified by names given them by the original settlers. Anyone familiar with the American Thanksgiving story knows that early European settlers owed a great debt to the Native Americans. From them, the colonists learned of different crops and foods and new ways of using the land and its resources. Canoes and kayaks have become popular recreational watercraft, and throughout much of Northern America, various ruins and other historical sites serve as important links to the region's first cultures and their important legacy.

DID A BULL CHANGE HISTORY?

Today, tourists can visit a reconstructed Viking settlement at L'Anse aux Meadows, a National Historic Site on the northern tip of Newfoundland. Here, according to ancient sagas (stories), a group of 160 Norse men and women from Greenland settled in the summer of 1003. In "Vineland the Good," they established a village called Hop under the leadership of Thorfinn Karlsefni. The Vikings had escaped the cold of Greenland and planned to start a permanent colony in this new land that offered great abundance. They even brought livestock, including Karlsefni's bull.

The Vikings met and began to trade with a group of people who arrived by canoe. They called these strangers *skraelings*. Things seemed to go well, until one day Karlsefni's bull suddenly charged from the forest. The skraelings, who had never seen cattle, fled in terror. They soon returned and attacked the Vikings, killing several and injuring others. The Norse soon realized that they were outnumbered and would never be safe in Vineland. They decided to abandon Hop and return to

Greenland, thereby ending the Norse attempt to settle North America. Karlsefni's enraged bull evidently delayed the permanent European settlement of the Americas for some 500 years! How different might Northern America's history and culture have been had it not been for one bull?

EARLY EUROPEAN EXPLORATION

European exploration of Northern America began in earnest approximately 500 years ago. Beginning with Columbus's voyage in 1492, European navigators began to sail westward in search of an all-water route to the Orient and its fabulous riches. The quest drew explorers from Italy, Spain, France, Portugal, the Netherlands and Great Britain across the Atlantic to the shores of the newly found land that, by 1507, had been named "America."

Sailing across the Atlantic in 1497, Giovanni Caboto, known as John Cabot, explored under the orders of King Henry VII of England. His mission was to find a new trade route to the Orient for the ever-expanding British empire. What Cabot discovered instead was perhaps the world's richest fishing grounds, which lay off of the eastern shore of Canada. When news of the cod-rich waters of the Grand Banks reached the king's ears, more ships departed. Soon, a thriving fishing industry developed on the eastern coast. This was the first of many instances in which Northern America's rich natural resources affected its cultural history. Later, some vessels began to venture south into the Gulf of St. Lawrence. Here, Europeans came in contact with native people and fishing crews exchanged beads and other trinkets for furs. Little did they know at the time that this initial trading soon would develop into a valuable fur-trading network.

Kings and other leaders still were eager to find a water route through Northern America to the Orient's rich spice markets. Eventually, however, a shift in thinking renewed interest in Northern America's natural riches. Far to the south, in Latin

America, Spanish explorers had discovered huge deposits of gold and silver. Spurred by tales of the vast wealth in the New World, the King of France sent Florentine explorer Giovanni da Verrazano on a voyage of exploration in 1524. Verrazano landed on the coast of North Carolina and continued northward, supposedly to avoid conflict with the Spanish, who were already establishing claims in Florida. His voyage carried him along the eastern seaboard as far as Nova Scotia and Newfoundland. Verrazano, believed to be the first European to follow the coast of present-day New England, and his "discoveries" soon drew other explorers.

EUROPEAN ROOTS IN AMERICAN SOIL

During four voyages between 1534 and 1543, Jacques Cartier, also dispatched by France, gathered more documentation of the lands and people in this area. He also ventured into the interior of Canada. Cartier had located the inviting water highway of the St. Lawrence River, which promised a route westward to the Great Lakes. He hoped to discover precious metals such as silver and gold. Instead, he found a resource of comparable value in the region's abundant fur-bearing animals.

The French continued to stream farther inland to other areas of Northern America. Trading posts were established where valuable furs could be collected both from trappers and through trade with native peoples. Small settlements and fur-trading posts continued to expand along the St. Lawrence River, the Great Lakes, and south along the Mississippi River to the Gulf of Mexico. Fur-trapping routes, mapped with knowledge gained from the native populations, were developed by both French and British trappers. Expansion of the fur trade was pushed by fashionable European hat makers, who desired the furs for their customers. Population increased, and with the more permanent settlements came increased economic activity and, for some individuals, prosperity.

Northern America

This is a drawing of Quebec City from the 1800s. Today, Quebec City is a bustling urban center widely known for its "Old World" charm.

As trade expanded, so did the European populations in Northern America. The French secured their first foothold, Port Royal, in what is now Nova Scotia, in 1605, three years before Samuel de Champlain founded Quebec on the St. Lawrence River. To the south, along the eastern coast of the United States, English settlers established Jamestown (Virginia) in 1607. English Puritans settled at Plymouth (Massachusetts) in 1620 and from there spread throughout much of New England. Dutch, Scandinavian, and German settlers soon were added to the growing diversity of Northern America's cultural mosaic. An ethnic mix of farmers, merchants, and tradesmen colonized what would become known as New York and Pennsylvania. By the mid-1700s, these diverse peoples lived in a group of colonies under British control.

SPANISH CLAIMS

Northern American history often is told with a northwest European slant. It is important to remember that huge areas of what is now the United States were first explored and claimed by Spain. In fact, St. Augustine, now in Florida, was settled by Spaniards in 1565, four decades before the French and British established their first permanent settlements. In the Southwest, Santa Fe (New Mexico) was established as a capital in 1610, a decade before the Pilgrims landed at Plymouth Rock. Spanish territorial claims and cultural influence stretched from Florida across the South and Southwest to California. They also reached far inland to include much of the interior West. Spain and later Mexico eventually lost political control of these lands, but the Hispanic cultural imprint remains strong throughout much of that region.

THE PLANTATION SOUTH

In the American South, ample moisture and a long, hot growing season were favorable for cultivation of plantation crops such as tobacco and cotton. North Europeans, primarily from the British Isles, were not accustomed to working in the sweltering heat and humidity, and Native Americans proved to be unsatisfactory as laborers. Throughout the seventeenth century, Europeans had brought a small number of Africans to America as slaves. African peoples were accustomed to hard work and steaming weather conditions, and they became able field hands. For more than a century, the South's plantation economy thrived, carried—literally—on the backs of slave laborers. Although the slave trade became illegal by 1808, the use of slaves as laborers was not terminated until 1863. By that time, several hundred thousand Africans had been added to the growing population. Yet another piece had been added to Northern America's richly diverse human mosaic.

STRUGGLES FOR WEALTH AND POWER

Even with the economic support of the fur trade, the French and British relied heavily on their mother countries both politically and militarily. Inevitably, the French and British struggled to control colonial lands in Northern America. This disruption caused much conflict between the French and British colonists, particularly along the eastern coastlands of Northern America during the 1700s and early 1800s.

As European settlement and political control spread, so, too, did European diseases and critical disruptions of native ways of life. In many areas, native populations were decimated and their lands taken, often by force. This loss of native people and their traditional ways of living altered the cultural history of Northern America. Coastal fishing peoples, eastern woodland farming cultures, southwestern pueblo dwellers, plains bison hunters, and northern Indian and Arctic Inuit families were forever changed by the "Angloization" of Northern America.

NORTHERN AMERICA MOVES WESTWARD

What began as a trickle of movement westward from the well-established east coast and St. Lawrence Valley settlements became a flood by the early 1800s. Land-hungry pioneers spilled across the Appalachian Mountains into the Ohio Valley and beyond. The interior valleys and plains were seen as a fertile farming frontier for hundreds of thousands of European immigrants. Scandinavian and German settlers were familiar with woodland living. They were skilled axmen who could use the forest resources to build sturdy log homes and fences and could clear land to farm. Rivers, the Great Lakes, and, later, canals provided vital transportation links.

By the mid-1800s, two events stimulated a rush across the continent. In the United States, gold was discovered in 1848 at a site in the western foothills of the Sierra Nevada east of San Francisco. The following year, tens of thousands of optimistic gold-seekers—the "49ers"—rushed across the continent in hope of finding their fortune. At the time, Russians had established a toehold along the California coast north of San Francisco. With their position threatened by the sudden explosion

Historical Geography

The first train between Montreal and the British Columbia coast is pictured in this 1886 photograph. The railroads were pivotal to westward expansion in Northern America.

of settlers, they withdrew to western Canada and eventually to Alaska. Finally, with the American purchase of Alaska in 1867, the Russians left Northern America.

With large populations now established on both coasts, the nation's attention turned to the need to link them with a safe and rapid means of transportation—the railroad. Trips by wagon were long, difficult, and very dangerous; so, too, was travel by water around the tip of South America or to Panama and then across the isthmus by land and northward to California by sea. In 1869, at Promontory Summit, a point just north of Utah's Great Salt Lake, tracks of the Union Pacific met those laid by workers for the Central Pacific. Completion of the world's first transcontinental railroad was celebrated with the driving of the final "Golden Spike."

Westward expansion also occurred in Canada, where settlers were first attracted to the fertile farmlands in southern Ontario. Agricultural expansion in Canada moved at a slower pace than in the United States, in part because of soil differences, a cooler climate, and a shorter growing season. The vision of two individuals greatly accelerated the pace of westward migration. The transcontinental railroad, the dream of Canada's first prime minister, Sir John A. Macdonald, was completed in 1885. As was the case in the United States, Chinese workers provided much of the labor. Descendents of these laborers established substantial Chinese communities in many U.S. and Canadian cities. Another important development was the introduction of Marquis wheat by Sir Charles Saunders in 1903. This strain of wheat was very well suited to Canada's shorter growing season and also could resist the strong winds that blow endlessly across the prairies. Just as the rails drew immigrants westward, so did this well-adapted crop. Thousands of people began to move into the interior to profit from agricultural expansion. Villages and towns bustled with growth as land rushes and westward expansion occurred in Northern America.

The excitement of seeking new lands and opportunities was interrupted by the struggles of two world wars and the Great Depression. World War I (1914–1918) and II (1941–1945) called for courage from Northern American citizens. They responded vigorously, contributing both natural and human resources to the military effort. The Dust Bowl and Great Depression of the 1930s also were tests of courage. Fortunately, urban and industrialized Northern America had beckoned millions of new immigrants whose courage and strength proved to be a blessing during this difficult time.

CREATING A NEW CULTURE REALM

Seeking new lands, resources, and opportunities, Europeans transformed the cultural landscape of Northern America. The region is held together by a net of culture history. Key elements include European colonization, immigration, and cultural diffusion that included shared beliefs in representative democracy, individual freedoms, and a market economy. Today, there are signs that the net may be fraying, allowing certain interests to slip through. In Canada, political tensions between French-speaking Quebec and her English-speaking provincial neighbors often reach the boiling point. Native peoples are involved in treaty disputes with both the U.S. and Canadian governments. Today, the traditional Anglo-European flavor of Northern America's culture is being further challenged. Both Canada and the United States are magnet destinations, attracting millions of immigrants, both legal and undocumented. Perhaps California offers a sneak preview of this region's future: More than half of the state's residents are now of a background other than Anglo (northwestern) European.

For several centuries, the Northern American experience was marked by cultural assimilation. This includes the Africans who were brought to the New World involuntarily but gradually adopted a dominantly European lifestyle. Today, however, Northern America is becoming increasingly culturally diverse. Asian and Hispanic populations, for example, are rapidly expanding. Once again, we are offered an opportunity to redefine this relatively uniform, yet incredibly diverse, culture region.

Population and Settlement

Northern America occupies an area of roughly 7,500,000 square miles (19.5 million square kilometers) divided almost equally between Canada (3.85 million square miles; 10 million square kilometers) and the United States (3.7 million square miles; 9.6 million square kilometers). The population of both countries is increasing slowly, at a rate well below the world average of about 1.2 percent per year. People in both countries are generally well-off in terms of life quality, educational attainment and literacy, and life expectancy. The similarities cease here, however. There are nearly 10 Americans to every Canadian, resulting in a U.S. population and population density nearly 10 times greater than that of its northern neighbor.

Population and Settlement

In terms of space, natural resources, and people—human resources—Northern America is blessed in countless ways. Nearly all land is suitable for some type of economic development and thus human settlement. Natural resources have supported widespread settlement, economic growth, and the development of human resources at a level perhaps unmatched anyplace else in the world. Each of these factors plays an important role in both the demographics (statistical data that relate to the human population) and settlement (where people live) of Northern America.

NUMBERS AND THEIR MEANING

Both the United States and Canada undertake detailed censuses (the United States in '00 years and Canada in '01 and '06 years). A census is any country's single most important source for data about its people. It involves much more than a "head count"; rather, in Northern America, the census provides a detailed statistical profile about each country's population.

Northern America is home to some 330 million people, about 33 million Canadians and 297 million Americans (2005 data). Only the culture realm that encompasses Australia and the Pacific has fewer people. Population within the region is growing annually at a quite sustainable rate of just less than one percent. Only rapidly aging Europe has a lower rate of growth.

Few areas of comparable size have a population density lower than Northern America's 44 people per square mile (17 per square kilometer). Population density figures can be terribly misleading, however: Canada's density is just under 9 people per square mile (3.4 per square kilometer). As can be seen on The World at Night image, however, vast areas of the country have almost no people at all. Even the United States, with about 80 people per square mile (31 per square kilometer), does not have an evenly distributed population. Most Americans cling to the country's coasts, leaving much of the interior sparsely populated. In fact, 75 percent of all Northern Americans live on only

46 Northern America

This is a population map of Northern America. Notice the greatest concentration of people can be found on the coasts of the United States, especially from Washington, D.C., to Boston.

about 2 percent of the land area! Certainly, none of the foregoing information suggests a condition of overpopulation. Neither Canada nor the United States has too many people to be supported by available space and resources.

Other demographic data also provide important information about the region's population and trends. For example, the total fertility rate (the average number of children born to each woman during her lifetime) has slipped below the replacement level of 2.1. It is 2.0 in the United States and 1.5 in Canada. This means that, in a matter of decades, if the trend continues, the population of both countries will begin to decline unless it is maintained by immigration. Both countries do receive a substantial number of immigrants.

In terms of health and life expectancy, Northern Americans, on average, live 78 years, longer than people in any of the world's other cultural realms. The worldwide average is 67 years. Canadians have a slight edge over Americans, with a life expectancy of 80 years versus 78 years. In both countries, women outlive men by about five years. With declining births and ever-lengthening life expectancies, the median age (currently about 37 years in both countries) is rising rapidly. In fact, only a handful of other industrial countries such as Japan and several Western European states have an older population.

An aging population creates a number of problems. There are fewer people to enter the workforce, and as the population ages, it is particularly difficult to find people to fill entry-level and lower-paying jobs. An aging population also means more retirees, who have a greater need for medical and retirement facilities, and financial retirement packages. The most obvious solution to the problems imposed by an aging population is to increase immigration. Both countries are experiencing substantial net gains in immigration. This, however, can cause problems as well as solve them. According to census data, an estimated 11 million immigrants—nearly 3.7 percent of the country's total population—live in the United States illegally.

PEOPLE AS RESOURCES

People are any country's most important resource—at least, potentially. Populations differ greatly, however, in terms of education, health, and productivity. Northern America enjoys one of the world's highest rates of literacy. Fully 97 percent of the people in both Canada and the United States can read and write. A substantial percentage of people in both countries also have college degrees. A well-educated population is essential if a country is to succeed in a postindustrial economy marked by information exchange, skilled services, and taking advantage of global linkages.

Good health, too, is essential if people are going to make significant contributions to society. An aging population with a long life expectancy is an indicator of good health, as are low rates of infant mortality. In Northern America, infant mortality is about 6 per 1,000 annually, the lowest in any of the world's culture realms.

A healthy and well-educated population, supported by a strong work ethic and good government, will be highly productive. Certainly, Northern America is blessed with each of these conditions. It is little wonder that the region also enjoys the world's strongest economy as measured by productivity, per capita income, and purchasing power.

EARLY SETTLEMENT

"Settlement" refers to where people live and why they choose to live there. When Europeans arrived on the shores of Northern America, they reached a land already occupied for thousands of years. Generally speaking, the outcome of this clash of civilizations favored the more powerful Europeans. Native lands were claimed and settled at will by the newcomers.

Estimates vary greatly in regard to Northern America's population at the time of European contact. Some anthropologists believe that fewer than one million people occupied the area that is now Canada and the United States, whereas others have placed the figure as high as 18 million. It seems most likely that 3 to 5 million people inhabited this part of the "New World" by A.D. 1500. Disease, warfare, and other factors reduced this number to about 400,000 by 1900. Also, as the wave of newcomers engulfed their homelands, native peoples often were forced onto lands judged to be less desirable by Europeans.

The first permanent European settlers in Northern America came as two distinctly different groups. Spaniards settled in a band that stretched from Florida to California, and Northwest Europeans first settled along the eastern seaboard. The first permanent European settlement in Northern America was St. Augustine, Florida, founded in 1565 by Spaniards. During the first decade of the seventeenth century, French and British outposts were established along the East Coast in 1605 and 1607, respectively. By 1625, the Dutch had joined the feeding frenzy for land, founding New Amsterdam (now New York City) at the mouth of the Hudson River. Meanwhile, Spaniards were pushing into present day New Mexico. By 1610, they had established Santa Fe as the capital of their growing empire in the Upper Rio Grande region.

British economic interests focused primarily on fishing and timber cutting. The Grand Banks in the waters off of Newfoundland proved to be perhaps the world's richest fishing area. Inland from the coast, the region's vast dense forests were an economic blessing to people who came from a largely deforested homeland across the Atlantic. As a result, early settlements clung tightly to the coastal region. Soon after securing their foothold in the St. Lawrence Valley and part of eastern Canada that they named "Acadia" (Nova Scotia), they began to move inland. Many of the French settlers were attracted by the abundance of fur-bearing animals found in the interior of North America. Pelts such as beaver sold for a premium in European markets. Spanish settlement focused on California and the Southwest. Here, the Spaniards sought gold and religious converts to the Roman Catholic faith among the Pueblo and other native peoples.

The Castillo de San Marcos has stood in St. Augustine, Florida, since the 1600s. Although the Castillo has served a number of nations throughout its history, it has never been taken by military force.

EARLY MIGRATION AND SETTLEMENT

By 1700, Northern America was on the brink of what was to become the greatest mass migration in human history. Nearly 50 million people are believed to have immigrated to the United States and Canada during a 250-year period. They came for many reasons. Some sought new lives, lands, and opportunities. Others were escaping oppression for their religious, political, or other views considered unpopular by the dominant population in their homeland. Some came unwillingly as slaves.

Most immigrants came from Europe. During the eighteenth century and the first half of the nineteenth, the British Isles were the primary source of immigrants for both the United States and Canada. More than one million Irish came to America during the potato famine of the mid-1800s alone. Among early immigrants, Germans ranked a close second. Newcomers from Scandinavia, Eastern Europe (including Russia), and Italy numbered in the millions.

In the southern United States, a growing plantation economy dependent on extensive hand labor thrived. Throughout tropical and subtropical areas of the Americas, this need was filled by Africans brought to the New World as slaves. Actual numbers of slaves taken from Africa are unknown. The most reasonable figures appear to be in the range of 9 to 10 million. Of this total, only about 6 percent were brought to the United States (540,000 to 600,000). Asians, particularly Chinese, also came. Most of them initially settled in cities on the West Coast. Eventually, however, Asians became the chief labor force in building the western segments of the transcontinental railroads.

Wherever newcomers settled, they introduced their culture, a process called "relocation diffusion." Northern America's population was growing numerically. It was also accepting and absorbing people of vastly different cultures on a scale never before experienced in human history. With few exceptions, people shed many traits of their cultural past and melded into the emerging Northern American way of life. In this "melting pot" process, a wonderfully diverse cultural mosaic was fashioned. Northern American culture was forged from the contributions of many others. (A hint of this rich diversity is suggested by a random scan of word origins in any good English dictionary.)

In terms of migration, early nineteenth-century New York City newspaperman Horace Greeley recognized future opportunity by urging, "Go West, young man, go West!" By the millions, people in both the United States and Canada heeded Greeley's advice. Nearly 200 years later, they continue to do so. In 1790, the center of the U.S. population was in northeastern Maryland, east of Chesapeake Bay. By 2000, it had moved to southeastern Missouri. Canada's population, too, has moved westward through time. One interesting fact about Canada's population is that the majority of Canadians live at the same latitude as Michigan and

Besides being the financial and business capital of the world, New York City has long been the United States' main gateway for immigrants from all over the world. More than 22 million immigrants entered the country through Ellis Island before it closed in 1954.

South Dakota! Only about 25 percent of them reside north of the 49th parallel of latitude, which forms the boundary between the western part of Canada and the United States.

Gold was the primary magnet that first drew adventurers westward across the continent. The 1848 discovery of this precious metal in California drew tens of thousands of fortune seekers to the "Golden State." Once settlement was established and gained momentum on the West Coast, particularly in San Francisco, others followed. During the latter half of the nineteenth century, Canada also experienced several gold strikes, which resulted in rushes that drew thousands of gold-hungry prospectors westward.

Whether "transportation follows people" or "people follow transportation" depends on circumstances. Obviously, both occur and are important for settlement. Generally speaking, people hesitate to settle in areas that are not linked to other places by transportation facilities. Coastal settlements had access to the sea and shipping routes, but a vast distance and incredibly difficult journey—overland or thousands of miles by water—separated the established settlements in the east from growing populations in the west. With few exceptions, the entire vast interior of the continent was all but void of European settlers. Visionary leaders began to call for the building of a transcontinental railroad.

By 1869, rails spanned the United States to link thriving San Francisco with major East Coast cities. By 1885, Canada completed its transcontinental route. Beginning in Halifax, Nova Scotia, rails snaked westward, passing through Montreal and Winnipeg and across the Prairie Provinces to Calgary. From there, they crossed the rugged Rocky Mountains and stretched to Vancouver, Canada's largest West Coast city. In both instances, governments and companies saw the need to attract settlers. Railroad companies were given land to help support the cost of building. Later, they established hundreds of communities along their tracks in hope of financially supporting their operations. As the rail network grew, settlement followed. Soon, the dawn of the automotive age further improved access. By the early twentieth century, European settlement had spread to all areas of Northern America, with the exception of a few very cold and extremely remote areas in the far north.

THE IMPORTANCE OF LOCATION

As anyone involved in real estate knows, location is perhaps the single most important factor in determining where people choose to settle. Whether as individuals or groups, people do not decide willy-nilly to simply "stop here." They select a location that is to become their home for a reason. Traditionally, economic factors—the ability to make a living by any means—have been the chief determinants of where people settle. Settlers sought well-protected harbors, good farm land, lakeshores or rivers that offered waterpower potential and access, or sites that offered mineral or some other resource wealth. Later, railroads, highways, and growing industrial centers that offered jobs all drew settlers. As culture and technology have changed, so too have perceptions of "ideal" places to live. In neither Canada nor the United States are population and settlement spread evenly across the land. What factors can help explain this seemingly strange pattern?

The Attraction of Water

As can be seen on the "nighttime" map and map of population density (page 46), Northern Americans have a strong preference for living near water. In fact, more than 80 percent of them live within 200 miles of the Atlantic or Pacific Ocean, the Great Lakes, or a major navigable river such as the Mississippi or St. Lawrence. Water, of course, is essential to life. It is also important for transportation, irrigation, and industry. More recently, people have flocked to seacoasts and lakeshores because of the scenic landscape they offer. The importance of water features is often suggested by a settlement's name. Many communities include within their name environmental terms such as "Harbor," "River," "Lake," "Falls," "Rapids," "Springs," or "Beach." Others suggest the use of water features, such as "Port," "Mill," or "Well."

In both Canada and the United States, most large cities were initially established and ultimately thrived because of their function as ports. On the Atlantic Coast, Boston, New York, Philadelphia, Charleston, Savannah, Jacksonville, and Miami grew as major port cities. Along the Pacific Coast, San Diego, San Francisco, Seattle, and Vancouver owed much of their success to this function. Toronto, Chicago, Milwaukee, Detroit, Cleveland, and Buffalo all grew as inland ports on the Great Lakes.

Inland, water routes also played a major role in the growth of many cities. Quebec City and Montreal thrived as Canadian ports on the St. Lawrence River. Minneapolis–St. Paul, St. Louis, Memphis, and New Orleans grew as ports on the Mississippi. Kansas City and Omaha prospered along the Missouri River, as did Cincinnati and Pittsburgh on the Ohio. Portland, Oregon, is located at the juncture of the Willamette and Columbia rivers. Hundreds of smaller communities throughout the United States and Canada also have benefited from their riverside locations.

In the dry western interior and throughout much of California, most settlement—both past and present—has depended on the availability of water. A detailed map reveals that nearly all communities within this region were located on streams. Chief exceptions include some mining communities and railroad centers. In some areas, local water sources were inadequate to provide for booming populations, and even today, much of southern California receives its water supply from elsewhere. Sustaining population growth in this region is much like someone on a life-support system. Aqueducts that serve as thin lifelines bring water from distant sources that include the northern Sierra Nevada range and the Colorado River. In the Southwest, Phoenix, Tucson, and Las Vegas rank among Northern America's most rapidly growing urban centers. Much of their growth depends on water diverted from the Colorado River.

In the future, water surely will become an increasingly important factor in the region's settlement. As regions within the United States begin to grow beyond their available water supplies, they will have to look elsewhere. Water, in fact, is perhaps the single most important natural limit imposed on population growth and settlement within the region.

Fertile Farmland

Northern America offers some of the world's finest farmland. Good soils, flat land, and adequate moisture are essential for successful farming. Once settlement moved inland from the coast, farmland was the primary attraction. Rich alluvial (stream-deposited) soils drew settlers across the broad Atlantic and Gulf coastal plains and into the interior river valleys and basins. In the mid-nineteenth century, the Homestead Act offered free land to people willing to settle and develop it. This lure drew hundreds of thousands of people into the interior United States. Later, the westward migration continued as people were attracted to the Central Valley of California, Oregon's Willamette Valley, Washington's Puget Sound region, and the Fraser River Valley in southern British Columbia. The last "agricultural frontier" was the vast interior plains. In both the United States and Canada, much of this area was not settled by large numbers of people until the latter part of the nineteenth century. The land could not be farmed until the steel-tipped moldboard plow was developed. This sharp-tipped, curved-surface plow could break through the thick prairie sod and turn the soil so that it could be tilled.

Improved Access

Throughout much of Northern America, railroads proved to be the primary magnets for settlement. In fact, in the vast region between the Rocky Mountains and the Appalachians, an estimated 80 percent of all communities can attribute their origin to railroads. Look closely at a detailed highway map that shows states or provinces east of a line that roughly coincides with the 100th meridian. (West of this, less than 20 inches [50 centimeters] of precipitation falls annually, thereby limiting agricultural potential). You will note that small towns are spaced at intervals of about 6 to 8 miles. A farmer could travel to town and back by horse-pulled wagon in one day if the community was no more than about 3.5 miles (5.6 kilometers) from a place of residence. Every 40 to 70 miles along the railroad is a larger population center. This pattern is not random. Railroads, hoping to profit from the sale of town lots and from serving the needs of surrounding farmers, located communities at the 6- to

Population and Settlement

8-mile interval. The larger communities served regional market functions and also as service centers for engines and other railroad equipment. Many large cities, such as Winnipeg, Chicago, and St. Louis, also grew as major centers based primarily on rail transportation.

Automobiles and roadways became a major factor of settlement in the early twentieth century. With few exceptions, it can be said that "people followed the railroads, but highways followed people." At the outset, at least, the building of railroads was a national task that served national needs. Building roads, on the other hand, was primarily a local (state, province, or community) task. Roadways thus were built in response to local needs. As the demand for fast and easy access grew, highways expanded to meet the need. In the 1950s, the United States began to develop an interstate highway system. Few government decisions have been more beneficial for commerce and travelers. In terms of contemporary population and settlement, the interstate system plays a major role. Most communities along these highways are stable or growing, and many towns and cities that were bypassed by the interstate system are declining in population.

Other Factors That Influence Settlement

Numerous other factors influence where people settle. Many early settlements, particularly in the arid and mountainous west, sprouted where ores were found. They boomed as mining centers and withered away as the minerals played out. Some coastal communities grew as fishing centers, and, in the interior, others thrived on logging. Although most such settlements underwent a boom-and-bust cycle, a number of them are once again thriving. They have become tourist centers that focus on scenery, local history, recreation, or some other modern attraction.

In both Canada and the United States, several hundred communities include "Fort" in their name, attesting to their (often

Ottawa began as Bytown, a logging community at the convergence of three rivers. It became the city of Ottawa in 1855 and was named the Canadian capital on December 31, 1857, by Queen Victoria.

former) strategic importance. Some cities, including Washington, D.C., and Ottawa, Ontario, Canada, were developed as centers of government. Certainly, many state and provincial capitals, as well as county seats, grew because of their government functions. Some towns flourish as university centers or centers for scientific research. Increasingly throughout Northern America, many communities depend on tourism as their primary source of revenue and hence, population growth.

CHANGING PATTERNS OF SETTLEMENT

Peoples' perceptions of "good" and "bad" places to live are based on their culture—particularly, how they make a living. During the past half-century, significant changes in culture have had a major effect on settlement patterns.

Rural to Urban

During the past century, millions of people have moved from the country to the city. Today, in fact, nearly 80 percent of all Northern Americans live in a metropolitan area. This rural-to-urban migration began with the shift from a self-sufficient folk culture and economy to a specialized popular culture based on a cash economy. Simply stated, people no longer could make an adequate living from a small plot of land; therefore, they moved from the country to the city in search of wage-paying jobs. Cities also offered many amenities other than jobs: better education, health care, entertainment, shopping, and many other activities and services. As industrial cities grew, so did the need for services. Educators, physicians, nurses, and attorneys were needed, and so were people involved in business, transportation, entertainment, and many other lines of work. As centers of industry, commerce, and services, New York, Chicago, and Los Angeles exploded in population to become some of the world's largest cities. In Canada, Toronto and Montreal also thrived.

Urban to Suburban

With the development of improved transportation facilities, people no longer needed to live near their place of work. They could move to the edge of the city and still work in town. Suburbia—smaller towns on the edges of cities—began to grow. Suburbs offered a more "natural" landscape with more space and greenery. They also were remote from the growing decay, congestion, and other problems associated with the inner city. Many people, however, soon came to realize that suburban life was rather "sterile." The "action" was in the city itself. There were other problems associated with suburban living, as well.

Anyone familiar with both Canadian and American cities cannot help but notice some major differences between them. Quebec City, Montreal, Ottawa, Toronto, and Vancouver are constantly ranked among the world's finest urban centers.

Meanwhile, to the south, cities such as Detroit, Cleveland, Buffalo, and Rochester suffer from urban blight and other problems common to many, if not most, American cities. How can these sharp differences be explained? The answer lies in different government policies. In the United States, many people live in suburbs and work in the inner city but pay property, sales, and other taxes to their suburban community. The inner city, strapped for revenue, is unable to provide adequate services or maintain its infrastructure. In Canada, on the other hand, taxes go to benefit the entire metropolitan area (a city and its suburbs). Under this arrangement, cities have adequate funds to support urban needs.

"Snowbelt" to "Sunbelt"

During the latter half of the twentieth century, millions of people left the industrial northeastern United States (the "Snowbelt" or "Rustbelt") and moved to the warmer South and Southwest (the "Sunbelt"). Climate alone cannot account for this major shift settlement. Many other factors were involved. Property, taxes, and other costs of living were very high in the North relative to the Sunbelt. Many northern cities were becoming dilapidated and factories obsolete. Wages were high, but most services were increasingly expensive. The Sunbelt, a region that extends from Virginia to California, offered relief from these conditions. Ultimately, however, a single technological innovation proved to be most responsible for this major shift: The air-conditioner made it possible for people to live comfortably in the Sunbelt's often scorching temperatures. It was not until effective and relatively inexpensive air-conditioning became available in the 1960s that the region's population began to explode.

"Must" to "Want"

During recent decades, yet another major change has occurred in regard to where Northern Americans decide to settle. In times past, most people's place of residence was determined by where they *must* reside in order to make a living. Most jobs were in industrial centers and so were most people. Today, many people hold jobs that make it possible for them to live where they *want* to reside. Society has moved from an industrial to a postindustrial service- and information-based economy. This means that millions of Americans and Canadians can "do their job" someplace other than in an urban factory or office. In addition, millions of retirees have adequate financial resources to retire to a location of their choice. Geographers refer to these new destinations as "amenity" locations—places that people choose because of scenery, climate, size, recreational opportunities, or some other factor.

The impact of this recent change in circumstances has been profound. Half a century ago, outside of major port cities, most coastal regions supported a small and dwindling population. The Appalachians and Ozarks were considered by many to be home to isolated and culturally-deprived "hillbillies." Former mining towns were seen as decaying "ghost towns" with dusty streets and abandoned buildings. Today, however, many such areas are booming and property values have become some of the nation's highest. Improved transportation, a society no longer tied to urban employment, and retirees who can live where they like have turned such areas into desirable amenity locations.

WHAT DOES THE FUTURE HOLD?

For several decades, Northern America's population has grown primarily because of immigration. With immigration comes both demographic and cultural change. In 2000, Hispanics squeezed ahead of blacks as America's dominant minority. In Canada, an Asian cultural imprint is widespread, particularly in Vancouver, Toronto, and other large urban centers. Migration certainly will continue in both countries, resulting in further social and cultural changes.

Fortunately, available space, good government, and a strong economy should allow Northern America to accommodate future population growth with minimal disruption. It is more difficult to estimate where population will decline or grow. There are signs that urban renewal is beginning to attract people back into American inner cities. Both the United States and Canada have huge areas of unsettled land. Canada's Maritime Provinces offer tremendous natural beauty, as do portions of the country's interior west. Isolation and a lack of economic development must be overcome if these areas are to develop. The U.S. interior plains and lowlands also offer many attractive settlement options. One thing is certain. Fifty years from now, statistical data and maps of population, settlement, and ethnicity will be different—perhaps surprisingly so—from those that show today's patterns of population and settlement.

CHAPTER 5

Culture and Society

Geographers have found that a people's way of life, or culture, is perhaps the most meaningful way to divide the world into regions. Also important is its society, how people interact with one another individually and as groups. Whether a society is cohesive and cooperative or divided and divisive is extremely important to cultural and social stability. Cultures are drawn together by shared symbols (such as languages, flags, and religious figures), common values, and similar historical experiences. In this chapter, you will learn about the ways in which diverse peoples have forged a relatively unified Northern American culture realm.

FLAGS AS SYMBOLS OF UNITY

Symbols are images that represent an object, an idea, or even a country. In order for them to be understood and appreciated, they must be placed within their cultural context. Consider the Canadian flag, with its red rectangular ends on either side of the single red maple leaf standing proudly in a white center rectangle. You know that in terms of Canada's European history, the British and French were the most important players. The flag's design shows no allegiance to either country, despite the role each has played. In regard to the maple leaf, long before the first Europeans arrived, native peoples knew of the sweet bounty of maple sap collected each spring from the sugar maple. Because of the tree's importance as a source of sugar, the maple leaf began to serve as an unofficial symbol of Canada as early as the 1700s. In 1965, when the current Canadian flag was first unfurled, thousands of Canadians gathered in Ottawa to witness the event. When presented, it was stated that the flag was a symbol of the nation's unity, for it represented all citizens of Canada without distinction of race, language, belief, or opinions.

The American flag also is rich in symbolism. The 13 stripes represent the original thirteen colonies that joined to form the United States of America. The 50 stars each represent a state in the union. As symbols, flags "stand" for the countries that they represent. As a result, much political action is strongly linked to the representative symbols. Americans and Canadians display their flags as symbols of national pride. Individuals who strongly disagree with national policy also may vent their anger using the nation's flag.

LANGUAGE: TIE THAT BINDS OR WEDGE THAT SEPARATES?

Language is perhaps the single most important "glue" that bonds any culture. Throughout the world, most countries with a common tongue are unified and harmonious. When a country is divided by language, dissension and conflict are common.

Europeans came to Northern America from many countries; thus, they spoke a babel of tongues. In the United States, despite the fact that most immigrants came from German-speaking roots, English ultimately became the dominant language.

The two countries within Northern America share many common experiences: European exploration and settlement, waves of immigration, westward expansion, and a tradition of democracy and individual freedom. There are some noteworthy exceptions to this commonality, however. One difference is the ongoing issue of French-speaking Quebec; another is the formation of Canada's native-governed territory of Nunavut.

French Quebec

Does language isolate its speakers? Does it unify its speakers? French and English are both official languages in Canada, but French is spoken almost exclusively in Quebec. Within the province, many Quebecois (French speakers who live in Quebec) fiercely believe that language unifies them and allows them to preserve their culture. Nearly 80 percent of the province's residents speak French as their first language. This language dominance is represented with pride in Quebec's media, heroes, and arts. Some French Canadians who live in Quebec feel that seceding (separating from the rest of Canada) is the best way to preserve their cultural heritage. Other French Canadians and most English speakers wish for all ten provinces and three territories in the country to remain united. They, along with the First Nations Cree of northern Quebec, who would also be affected by secession, oppose separatism. This divisive issue continues to make newspaper headlines regularly.

The Inuit and Nunavut

Culture-based separatism is alive and well elsewhere in Canada. In 1999, the country's Inuktitut-speaking Inuit (Eskimo) people were granted Canada's third and newest territory— Nunavut. Its population is largely Inuit, the indigenous peoples

66 Northern American

The flags of Canada's ten provinces and three territories are displayed on this stage during a ceremony to mark the birth of the new Canadian territory of Nunavut, April 1, 1999.

who have lived there for several thousand years. The harshness of the remote land they now govern is suggested by the fact the Inuit language has more than 40 descriptive words for snow and ice! In this endless, windswept region of the far north, 28,000 residents occupy an area that of about 735,000 square miles (1,900,000 square kilometers), roughly one-fifth of Canada's entire landmass. Within this vast area, there are only about 30 communities that range in population from a few dozen to about 6,000 living in Iqaluit, the capital city located on remote Baffin Island.

Inuit cultural values and beliefs are recognized by the Canadian government as Nunavut strives to make this governing process succeed. Cultural, social, and political challenges are being addressed with the determination to maintain and hopefully increase the population scattered across this territory.

Nunavut faces many critical challenges, however. Its people are learning that there is a high cost to preserving a minority culture. Unemployment is widespread, levels of education are low, and suicide rates are alarmingly high. Substance abuse is rampant, the cost of goods is astronomical (the equivalent of about ten U.S. dollars for one gallon of milk), and public services are poor to nonexistent. No road, railroad, or scheduled airline service connects the territory to any outside location.

Many people in Canada and elsewhere wonder whether Nunavut will become a successful model for other indigenous groups that wish to become self-governing. Some fear that the experiment will ultimately spotlight the folly of culture-based politics that lead to self-government. Nunavut has been in place only since 1999, and its outcome remains in doubt.

Language, Diversity, and Stability in the United States

"Becoming American" has always been the key to achieving individual success in the United States. The most important step in this process has always been learning English. Nearly all socially, economically, and politically successful Americans were and continue to be English speakers. According to recent census data, however, the number of families that do not speak English as their first language is increasing rapidly. In a country that has become accustomed to the "celebration of diversity," cultural differences can and should be accepted. Many, however, question whether non-English speakers will be able to compete successfully in the dominant English-speaking society. Others suggest that the rapid increase in Spanish-speaking people in the United States is a prelude to cultural conflict. They need only point to Canada and the problems that have resulted from its linguistic divisions.

FREEDOM TO WORSHIP

Many early European settlers of Northern America came because they suffered religious persecution in their homelands.

68 Northern American

Youths wave flags for Pope John Paul II at the papal welcoming ceremony in Toronto, July 25, 2002. The pope visited Toronto for the seventeenth annual World Youth Day.

The New World offered freedom of worship; it was a place where groups such as the Puritans and Pilgrims could practice their faith without fear of reprisal. Ultimately, the religious makeup of Northern America became as diverse as the many faces of its population.

The majority of Northern Americans—75 to 80 percent—claim a form of Christianity as their faith. In the United States, Protestants outnumber Roman Catholics by a margin of about two to one. In Canada, Catholics slightly outnumber Protestants. With religious intolerance increasingly evident in various areas of the world, one statistic stands out in regard to Northern America: Nearly 3,000 different religious faiths are practiced! This amazing figure certainly spotlights the belief in an individual's fundamental right to freedom of worship.

Generally speaking, Northern America has been the world's most tolerant region in its acceptance of diverse religious beliefs. In addition to Christianity, some faiths, such as Judaism, have been here since the countries were founded. Others have arrived more recently. Islam, Buddhism, Hinduism, Sikhism, and several smaller religious sects have a million or more followers. The religious composition of Northern America will continue to mirror the growing diversity of beliefs within this culturally expansive region.

FOOD AND DIET

What people eat and drink is one of the most fundamental traits of any culture. Throughout much of the world, diets are unchanging: People eat the same foods prepared in the same way day after day throughout their lifetime.

Readers who enjoy a varied diet may consider themselves very fortunate. No place else in the world offers a greater variety of food and beverage options than Northern America. Few communities of any size are without a Mexican, Italian, or Chinese restaurant. Greek, French, Middle Eastern, Thai, Japanese, and other ethnic restaurants can be found in most middle-sized communities. Large cities, of course, offer a wonderful smorgasbord of food options.

Most of the world's people drink water and one other beverage on a regular basis. Think of the mealtime options available to Northern Americans: tea or coffee, beer or wine (in many different varieties), sodas of various flavors, milk (with various percentages of fat content) and, of course, water (tap or bottled). Most Northern Americans long ago gave up eating three meals a day. Which two are consumed? Some opt for breakfast and dinner (supper), whereas others eat lunch and the evening meal. There is even some confusion over the naming of our meals. Farm people generally refer to breakfast, dinner, and supper, whereas urbanites prefer breakfast, lunch, and dinner. Dinner usually is the largest meal of the day, traditionally consumed midday by farmers.

CULTURAL RELATIVITY AND CHANGE

Culture is a very relative thing. It is difficult, if not impossible, to "rank" people's ways of living. Some cultures, including Northern America, are highly ranked as measured by diverse technology, strong economy, huge vocabulary, and other measurable traits. Even so, many people who live in less-developed countries (LDCs) are dismayed over certain aspects of Northern American culture. They are often shocked over the high divorce rate and the way senior citizens are treated. They cannot begin to comprehend the lack of respect shown by many youngsters toward their elders, and they resent the United States's "bully-of-the-block" approach to relationships with other countries.

Cultures, like all organisms, grow and change through time. This occurs in one of two ways: through local development (discovery, invention, or innovation) or by way of diffusion (the acceptance of traits that originated elsewhere). New traits can be developed anywhere. The Inuit igloo, for example, is one of the great architectural developments of all time and was the inspiration for the geodesic dome—yet it was first built in a very remote location. Generally speaking, however, cities have been the centers of culture change. In Northern America, most urban residents are formally educated and many hold advanced degrees or well-honed skills. Universities, research centers, great libraries, and industries that depend on innovation are found in most cities. A single technology such as the computer (developed in Northern America) can bring about huge change within a culture. Think of the countless ways in which we have come to depend on the computer and its many functions and how its use has changed our lives.

The second way in which culture changes is through diffusion, the movement of traits from elsewhere. Some traits are transferred by moving people. Europeans who came to America brought their ways of living with them. Northern American religion, language, market economy, and ideas about democracy and individual freedoms (and responsibilities) all originated in the Old World. So, too, are many crops and domesticated animals, preferred beverages and food staples, the idea of men wearing a tie, and the way the inner spaces of homes are built and divided. Because there are so many linkages to other lands and peoples, Northern Americans have benefited from diffusion as have no other people.

Cultures also change through time. Values change, technology changes, society changes. In a very fast-paced culture, many people find it difficult to keep up with the kaleidoscopic pace of changes. They are bewildered by CD players and televisions with 80 buttons and knobs, the computer and all of its functions, and the fast pace of scientific breakthroughs. With change, however, progress often comes. It is doubtful that many Northern Americans would want to return to the "good old days," which, in most respects, were rather bad.

THE EXPORT OF POPULAR CULTURE

Both authors have had the good fortune to experience considerable international travel, and they never cease to be amazed at the "imprint" of Northern American culture in even the most remote areas of the world. The American hamburger can be found almost everywhere beef is consumed. It can be washed down with an American soft drink as the diner listens to the latest popular song by an American artist. Blue jeans, American cigarettes, and motion pictures are almost everywhere. Fads that began in California, New York, or Aspen, Colorado, are rapidly adopted by youngsters worldwide.

Some cultures resent the widespread diffusion of Northern America's popular culture. Consumption of alcohol, scantily clad women, and displays of great wealth bother them, as do the lyrics of rap and other songs, the flood of American manufactured products, and the spread of many emerging social patterns. Can they be criticized for wanting to protect their values and way of life? This is a very important question. Increasingly, many people, including some Northern Americans, are worried about the process of "globalization," which includes the spread of Western culture. They see a bland future world in which Western economy, society, and values will prevail worldwide.

Cultural concerns exist even within Northern America. French Canadians proudly resist many Anglo culture traits, as do many indigenous peoples. In the United States, there are growing concerns over how best to accommodate the growing Hispanic population. At the country level, Canadians are often extremely critical of many aspects of U.S. culture that seep northward across the border. An overwhelming majority of Canada's population hugs the U.S. border. With this close proximity to the United States, Canadians are constantly bombarded by American popular culture. American-made products and chain retailers flood the Canadian market. American current events, magazines, television programming, movies, and sports are well-known in Canada and influence the lives of Canadians. With few exceptions, Canadian current events, media, and political developments rarely reach south of the border into the United States. With some exceptions, Canadian happenings tend not to have much effect on the daily lives of people who live in the United States. Helen Gordon McPherson once stated, "Canadians have been so busy explaining to the Americans that we aren't British, and to the British that we aren't Americans that we haven't had time to be Canadians!"

CHAPTER 6

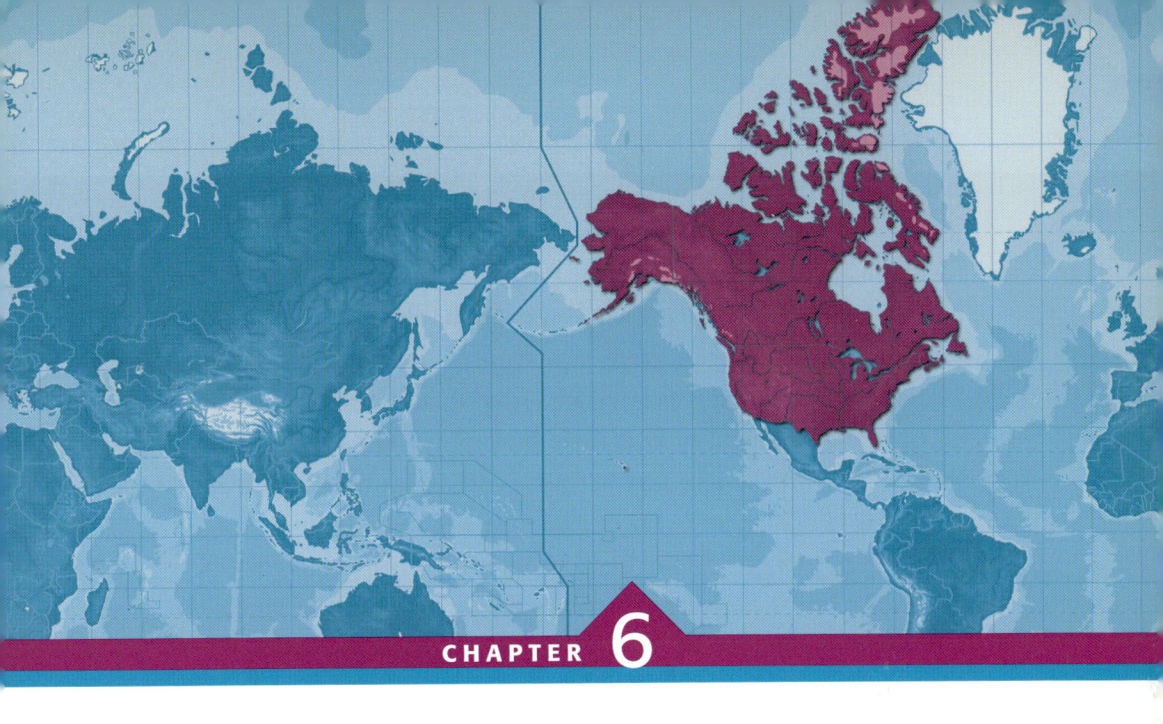

Political Geography

Good government may be the single most important factor in determining a country's well-being. Northern America, perhaps more than any other region, has been blessed with good governments. In this respect, its people and institutions have been extremely fortunate. Political geographers believe that a "good government" is one that achieves two vital goals: First, it protects its territory and population from foreign aggression; second, it allows its people and institutions to function in the most effective manner for the benefit of all citizens.

Think for a moment about the various ways in which political decisions affect your life. Each day, government—both directly and indirectly—has an impact on our lives in hundreds, if not thousands, of ways. Countless laws influence our actions. We benefit from postal services, law enforcement, and various social services such as health care and retirement programs. Nearly all roads and highways are built and maintained as public facilities, as are government buildings and many other structures. Government-imposed survey systems divide our land, and laws determine its ownership and, through zoning laws, often its use. Public lands—including forests, parks, monuments, and other areas—are set aside for our use and enjoyment. A strong military has protected Northern America from foreign invasion. Sadly, these blessings often are taken for granted. Many people simply do not realize how uniquely fortunate Canadians and Americans are! In this chapter, these and other important aspects of government are considered from the perspective of political geography.

NATION BUILDING

A country is much like an organism: It can grow, maintain, or wither. Some parts can be healthy and functioning while others are plagued with problems. Many changes occur over time. Both the United States and Canada began as relatively small footholds along their eastern margins. Eventually, they grew to span the North American continent from the Atlantic shore to the Pacific (and, in the case of Hawaii, far beyond). As pieces of a puzzle fall into place to create a complete picture, Northern America's two countries grew piece by piece.

The territorial expansion of present-day Canada began in 1867. In that year, a confederation (union) that included Ontario, Quebec, New Brunswick, and Nova Scotia, was formed. Three years later, in 1870, Manitoba and the Northwest Territories were added. A year later, British Columbia entered the federation; Prince Edward Island joined in 1873. In 1898, the remote Yukon region gained territory status within the confederation. The Prairie Provinces of Saskatchewan and Alberta were admitted in 1905. Finally, in 1949, ten years before Hawaii and Alaska gained statehood in the United States, Newfoundland and Labrador completed Canada's territorial expansion. Nunavut was granted territory status in 1999, but was created from the Northwest Territories that had been part of the union for more than a century.

Territorial growth within the United States was somewhat different than that of Canada. Pieces of the Canadian political puzzle were what became provinces or territories. The growth of the United States was by large areas that did not necessarily coincide with what became political boundaries. Land acquired by the Louisiana Purchase, for example, ultimately was divided into all or part of 15 states.

In 1776, the United States was composed of 13 former colonies. These lands extended from the Appalachian Mountains to the Atlantic Coast and from Maine to Georgia. By 1783, the country had pushed westward to include nearly all lands east of the Mississippi River. The vast interior of the United States was acquired in the Louisiana Purchase of 1803. Lands from Florida westward to Texas and a narrow strip that extended into Wyoming were gained from Spain between 1819 and 1845. The Pacific Northwest (Oregon Territory) was acquired in 1846, and most of the Southwest was gained in the Mexican Cession of 1846. In 1853, with the Gadsden Purchase, the territorial expanse occupied by the 48 U.S. states was completed.

Alaska was purchased from Russia in 1867 in what must rank as one of the greatest real estate bargains of all time—7.2 million dollars, or about two cents per acre (one cent per hectare)! At the time, most Americans were highly critical of the purchase, which earned the nickname "Seward's Folly," after U.S. Secretary of State William Henry Seward, who initiated the purchase. Today, Alaska produces more wealth in a single day than its original purchase price. Finally, Hawaii was annexed in 1898. Alaska and Hawaii did not achieve statehood until 1959—ten years after Canada's present-day political map was filled in.

In expanding their respective territories, both the United States and Canada had to overcome huge obstacles of distance, rugged terrain, and harsh climates (aridity in the United States and cold in Canada). Such physical handicaps were overcome by both countries' fierce desire to survive and expand as political units.

GOVERNMENTS

Political structure of the United States and Canada is similar in some ways, but quite different in others. One difference is that the United States became fully independent in 1776. Canada did not achieve the full power of self-government from Great Britain until 1982. Both countries, however, are strongly democratic, and both enjoy relative political stability. Both also have many layers of government that range in scope from national to state or provincial and down to the local level. In both countries, a federal system prevails in which constitutions grant states and provinces the right to share powers with the national governments. In Canada, considerable competition exists among the provinces and territories. In the competition for resources and local decision making, Canadian provinces are much more independent than are U.S. states. Ironically, Canada is often judged to be a "liberal" country, whereas the United States is more conservative.

The United States and Canada both have a constitutionally guaranteed balance of political power, with executive, legislative, and judicial branches of government. Here, the similarity begins to vanish. Whereas the United States has an elected president, Canada's chief of state is the British monarch, who is represented by a governor general. The Canadian head of government is the prime minister. Rather than being elected to office, the prime minister is appointed. After legislative elections, the majority party (or coalition of parties) leader in the House of Commons is automatically designated prime minister by the governor general.

Political Geography

U.S. President George W. Bush shakes hands with Canadian Prime Minister Paul Martin in the rotunda of Centre Block (the main building of Parliament) after signing the guest book on November 30, 2004, in Ottawa, Ontario, Canada.

Legislative branches of both governments function in a somewhat similar manner. In the United States, Congress is divided into two branches. The Senate has 100 members, two from each state, who are popularly elected to six-year terms. The House of Representatives has 435 members; each state's representation is based on its population. Members are elected to two-year terms. Canada's Parliament consists of a 105-member Senate and 308-seat House of Commons. Senators are appointed by the governor general, with the advice of the prime minister, and can serve until they reach 75 years of age. Members of the House of Commons are elected by direct, popular vote to serve terms of up to five years.

The judicial branch in each country is quite similar. Both have a Supreme Court and numerous levels of federal, state or provincial, and local courts. Of greatest importance to citizens of both countries are the constitutional guarantees to individual rights (and responsibilities) and freedoms. "Cussing the government" seems to be a popular parlor game throughout Northern America. As citizens, however, Northern Americans must remember that the government that they criticize also protects their right to criticize.

In terms of political stability, both countries have centrifugal forces—factors that tend to destabilize, or divide, a country. Canada has the deep division and often sharp conflict between its English-speaking population and French-speaking Quebec. As recently as 1995, a referendum on Quebec's independence failed to pass by only a very small margin. If the province achieved independence, Canada would become a physically divided country. The Maritime Provinces, in particular, would suffer politically and economically. Canada's native people constitute a third political-interest group. Nunavut already has gained territorial status as a native-governed (Inuit) political unit. Resource-rich and politically conservative Alberta becomes increasingly restless over what it perceives to be unfair treatment from Ottawa. Many Canadians feel a greater sense of "belonging" to their province than to their country.

In the United States, regional conflicts have not really boiled over since the Civil War of the 1860s. Many states, including remote Hawaii and Alaska, do not always feel that they are treated fairly by the federal government. Generally speaking, however, local grievances are issue related, rather than region based. The Pacific Northwest lumber industry, for example, suffered greatly from federal legislation that protects the endangered spotted owl.

GOVERNMENT, LAND, AND RESOURCES

Both the United States and Canada have vast areas of land. From the beginning, some lands were privately owned. Most land, though, is government owned. In the United States alone,

763 million acres (309 million hectares) of land is in the public domain. Government ownership of land reaches 90 percent in Alaska and Nevada. Obviously, an early and extremely important task of both governments was to establish a land policy: Who would own the land? How would it be acquired? How would land be divided (surveyed)? What controls would be placed on land use?

Today, public lands include vast areas of particularly sparsely populated Northern America. Such areas are often woodlands, mountainous terrain, or regions in which economic potential is limited by climatic conditions. In addition, there are national parks, monuments, wilderness areas, and Indian trust lands. Governments also have capitals, government buildings, transportation right of ways, and other facilities such as military bases.

Land survey systems, perhaps more than any other political element, create their own distinctive imprint on the landscape. Much of eastern Northern America has a very irregular survey pattern. Roads seem to wander, fields are irregular in shape, and little "order" is evident. This "random" pattern changed with the implementation of the rectangular survey system, adopted in the late eighteenth century. The Midwest, for example, resembles a checkerboard with roadways spaced at intervals of one mile. Fields are rectangular, and everything is neatly oriented in the cardinal directions. Elsewhere, Spanish land grants and the French long lot system also gave rise to distinctive land division patterns.

Many Europeans and others who travel in Northern America are surprised by the density of rural settlement. Throughout most of the world, rural people live in villages. As early as 1862 in the United States and 1872 in Canada, a quarter section (.25 square mile; .65 square kilometer) of land could be acquired for a minimal fee. Owners had to settle on and improve the land they claimed by building a house, farm, and fence, for example. In this way, rural settlement was scattered and economic development was more evenly distributed.

Governments also can control the use of land and other natural resources in many ways. Laws place restrictions on grazing, farming, logging, hunting and fishing, mining, and many other activities. Water and soil resources also are protected by both federal and local laws. Zoning restrictions prohibit certain land uses in urban areas. A factory or warehouse, for example, cannot be built in a residential area. Such restrictions are in place to protect people's health, economic, amenity, and other interests.

GOVERNMENT AND ECONOMY

In Northern America, a government-supported capitalist (free-market) economy has been the foundation of widespread prosperity. Governments play a vital role in economic development in many ways. Nearly all businesses, for example, depend on reliable transportation. Railroads were constructed with government support; highways, including the U.S. interstate system, were built and are maintained by local, state, and federal governments; and shipping and air traffic are government regulated.

As any farmer or rancher knows, the government plays a very important role in agriculture, including direct economic support in some instances. Industry, too, is both assisted and occasionally controlled by government. The government can provide incentives and support, such as building municipal industrial parks or offering tax benefits. It can also regulate businesses. If a business becomes a monopoly or threatens people's health or safety, the government will step in.

Having an ample supply of relatively inexpensive energy is essential to economic growth and development. In some ways, governments are directly involved in the production of energy, as is the case with huge hydroelectric dams. In most instances, government policy promotes and also regulates resource development, distribution, and cost.

Good government and a strong economy go hand in hand. In the following chapter, you will learn how Northern America has prospered economically.

CHAPTER 7

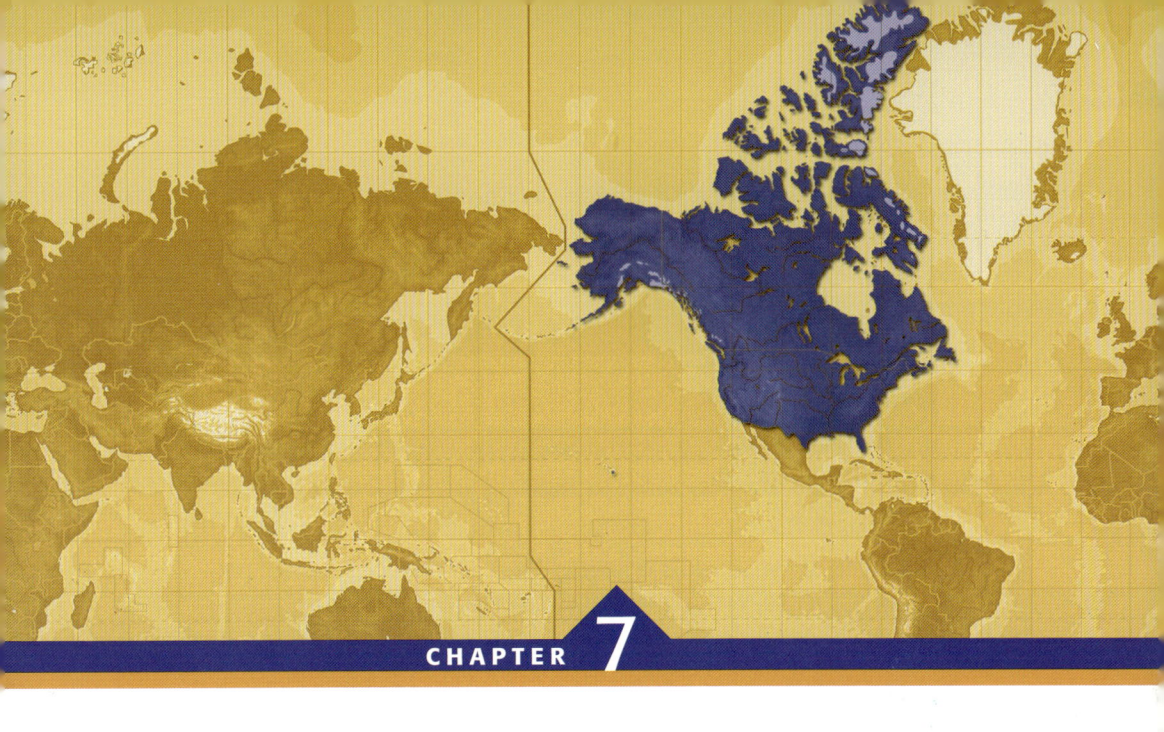

Economic Geography

"What career options would I have if I lived in Vancouver, Miami, Chicago, Toronto, or a less-populated area of Northern America?" "How do the forests, minerals, mountains, and fertile plains support not only people in Northern America, but also many throughout the world?" Questions such as these can best be answered by learning about a region's economic geography.

By nearly any measure, Northern America is the world's leading economic powerhouse. The combined annual gross domestic product (GDP) of the United States and Canada is nearly 13 trillion U.S. dollars (2005 estimate). This amounts to a staggering one-third of the total global value of production and services! California alone would be the world's fifth-ranking economic power if it were an independent country. This chapter explains the foundations that have contributed to the region's economic well-being.

Many factors contribute to a region's economic success, and Northern America possesses most, if not all, of them. Spatially, it occupies 13 percent of Earth's land surface, most of which has been or can be made productive in some way. In terms of trade, the region is strategically located between Western Europe and rapidly growing markets in Eastern Asia. It faces three of the world's oceans. These water bodies offer protection for the region's borders and provide easy access to global markets. The region has a cornucopia of resource wealth, including fuels, metals, forests, water, and many other essential elements. It also has a great diversity of terrain, climate, and ecosystems.

People, too, are resources, and Northern America is blessed with a healthy, well-educated, hard-working workforce. In addition, the region does not suffer from a condition of overpopulation. Ample space and other opportunities for future growth and development exist. Finally, a country's economic system—its means of production, variety and efficiency of services, and ways of distributing wealth—and government are keys to prosperity (or failure). Northern America has been blessed with strong market economies and stable governments. Businesses and individuals are free to pursue their economic interests with minimal governmental interference. In Northern America, the market itself determines what will be produced, in what quantities, and at what cost.

FOUNDATIONS OF ECONOMIC DEVELOPMENT

There is no assurance that vast land, abundant resources, or a large population will contribute to a region's economic prosperity. Many factors influence the nature and success of economic activity. Some are physical in nature and others historical, and, ultimately, all depend on a people's cultural system.

Natural Environment

The natural environment can provide a foundation for economic development. No area, regardless of its environment, lacks economic potential. Ultimately, however, people—their culture, technology, needs, and so forth—make things possible. (As a tourist, would you like to see Greenland's ice cap, watch polar bears along the shore of Hudson Bay, or visit a remote Inuit village?) Northern America's varied natural conditions, including climates, ecosystems, landforms, and natural resources, offer the widest possible range of economic activities. In Chapter 2, you learned that Northern America is the only region that includes all of the world's climates and ecosystems somewhere within its territory. Such diversity makes it possible to grow any of the world's crops or raise any breed of livestock. Other industries also are favored by varied environmental conditions. The logging industry depends on abundant forests resources, and fisheries depend on extensive marine resources. Many other industries are favored by environmental conditions, as well. The Sunbelt, for example, has attracted millions of people and billions of dollars because of its mild climate.

Northern America also benefits from varied terrain. Broad plains favor farming with large equipment, the construction of highways and railroads, and building homes, businesses, factories, and other structures. Towering mountain peaks attract skiers and many other tourists because of their deep winter snow, rugged beauty, and cool summer temperatures. Any crop can be grown and any activity pursued someplace in the region. Because of its environmental diversity, Northern America is the world's only potentially self-sufficient region.

The region's economy also benefits enormously from its wealth of natural resources. Fertile soils, vast forests, an abundant supply of surface and groundwater, and diverse wildlife have been important keys to economic development from the earliest period of European settlement. Mineral resources such as coal, petroleum, natural gas, and uranium have fueled economic de-

A farmer works in a field in Starks Corner, Quebec, Canada. Although agriculture is not the primary industry in Northern America, there are still large areas of agricultural land.

velopment. Abundant industrial metals such as iron ore, copper, and a wealth of other metalic minerals have spurred manufacturing. Gold and silver were of great economic and historical importance, particularly in the region's western interior.

Cultural Contributors to Economic Growth

A great number of cultural factors have contributed to Northern America's economic success. People of Northwest European culture tend to possess a strong "Protestant work ethic." In essence, this means that people are eager and willing to work and believe that working is honorable. Surprisingly, perhaps, only a small fraction of the world's people hold this view. Northern Europe also was home to and benefited greatly from the Industrial and Commercial revolutions. Manufacturing and selling—as well as serving those who do either—spread rapidly from the British Isles throughout much of Northern America. The idea of a market-based economy also diffused to the region from northwestern Europe. Northern America has long been a world leader in technology. The region is home to many of the world's most important ideas, tools and techniques, and skills. From the harnessing of electricity to development of the computer and the Internet, each innovation has helped the region's economy grow.

A well-integrated infrastructure is also an essential element of economic development. Northern America is served by an excellent network of railroads, highways, airways, pipelines, and other distribution networks. Only very sparsely populated areas of the western interior and far north remain relatively inaccessible. Finally, as previously mentioned, the region's political institutions and economic systems have played a vital role in fostering its economic prosperity. Generally speaking, they encourage and support the production, distribution, and services that are essential for economic stability.

In today's global economy, an understanding of geography is essential. People simply cannot compete successfully if they are geographically illiterate. To be successful economically, one must know much more than local environmental conditions, production, and sales. One must think globally. How can a freeze in Brazil affect the price of orange juice in Alaska? How does increasing prosperity in China mean higher gas prices at your local station? Why does an investor in Arizona keep a sharp eye on the day's stock market activity in Japan, elsewhere in Asia, and in major European countries? Can religion-based terrorist activity in Europe affect the economy in Toronto or Montreal? Can a weak South Asian monsoon that results in drought be a boon to wheat farmers in Montana and Saskatchewan? Has your community been hurt (or helped) by the practice of "outsourcing," in which a company looks abroad for less-expensive manufacturing and services? These are only a few examples of ways in which each individual and community in Northern America is closely linked to lands, peoples, conditions, and events worldwide.

CATEGORIES OF ECONOMIC ACTIVITY

Geographers divide economic activities in several ways. Perhaps the most commonly used method focuses on what people do in terms of complexity and involvement with the natural environment. Some jobs, such as mining, logging, farming, and fishing, require great skill and much physical labor but little formal education. Incomes of workers in these industries tend to be quite low. Jobs, and thus workers, are very much tied to one place. People involved in these "primary" industries often have a very limited awareness of the "outside" world. At the other extreme are people engaged in professional services, which includes executive decision makers and managers, educators and researchers, doctors and attorneys, and many others. These jobs require extensive formal education and considerable knowledge and skill. They generally pay quite well. People engaged in these activities have considerable mobility. Increasingly, they also must possess a detailed "mental map" of both the region and the world. Jet aircraft place nearly any destination within a day's reach. Computers and other instant communications have brought the world together as one giant neighborhood. The electronic expressway brings us instant communication and up-to-the-minute information from every corner of the planet. It has changed the way business is now done in the global marketplace.

Primary Industries

Primary industries are those that are directly involved with the exploitation of natural resources, such as agriculture, fishing, mining, and logging. Each of these industries is extractive in nature—things are taken from the land or sea. As a result, they have become increasingly pressured by environmental restrictions.

Economic Geography 87

This is a land use map of Northern America. Although large areas of land support primary industries, such as agriculture and logging, the majority of the population is involved in manufacturing, trade, or providing services.

Fewer than 5 percent of Northern Americans are engaged in primary industries today, and the number is rapidly declining.

Agriculture

Traditionally, agriculture has been the primary industry that involves the greatest number of people. Today, less than one percent of all Northern Americans are engaged in farming or ranching, yet those few people are the world's greatest producers of food, beverages, and fiber. Many factors have combined to help make this remarkable achievement possible. Much of the region has good soils. Climatic conditions, including moisture and an adequate growing season, are favorable (some hardy crops are grown as far north as Fairbanks, Alaska). Huge expanses of relatively flat land make the use of large mechanized equipment possible. The region also has benefited from its leadership role in agricultural research and technology. Although the number of farmers and ranchers has decreased, the average size of operations has greatly increased. In fact, production has never been higher.

Fishing

Waters that surround Northern America have provided an abundance of fish, crabs, shrimp, lobsters, oysters, and other valuable marine resources since the dawn of settlement. Because of overharvesting, particularly on Canada's Grand Banks, many commercially valuable species are becoming depleted. Today, some species, including salmon, shrimp, and oysters, are even "farmed." As the demand for seafood increases, harvests will decline unless appropriate steps are taken to conserve this important resource.

Mineral Extraction

Mining long has been and continues to be a very important contributor to Northern America's economy. In fact, some would argue that a wealth of mineral resources was the primary factor that contributed to the region's rise as the world's leading economic power. For two centuries, this region was self-sufficient in mineral fuels, with huge reserves of coal and, later, petroleum and natural gas. Metals such as iron and copper were found in huge deposits, as were other minerals essential for industrial growth. Only recently has the region had to begin to import certain minerals. Most critical to the region's future economic well-being is the increasing dependence on imported petroleum.

Logging

Lumber, pulp, paper, and other industrial products depend on the logging industry. Throughout much of Northern America, however, the industry is under attack. Forests once covered much of the Atlantic and Gulf coast regions inland to the Mississippi River and Lake Winnipeg. A broad band of forest spanned the northern part of the continent from Alaska to Canada's Atlantic shore. On the West Coast, dense forests of redwood, spruce, pine, and other valuable species extended from central California into the Alaskan panhandle. Today, much of the lumber-grade timber is gone. It has been used to build homes and other frame structures, railroad ties, and dozens of other important things that we take for granted. As natural woodlands are cut over, secondary growth (often planted, as in "tree plantations") is usually of lower quality. It can take decades or even centuries for trees to grow to a harvestable size.

Secondary Industries

Secondary industries manufacture or process primary materials in some way. They take natural resources or raw materials and turn them into something useful. Examples include manufacturing industries, building industries (using wood, stone, cement, or other earthen materials), and energy production. Smelting, refining, steelmaking, textile and clothing manufacturing, and chemical manufacturing all fall within this category, as do the automobile and aircraft industries. Today, much of the world's secondary economic activity is taking place in parts of the world where wages are low. The number of people engaged in secondary industries has declined sharply in Northern America, to less than 20 percent.

Tertiary and Other Related Activities

Today, nearly 80 percent of all employed Northern Americans are engaged in tertiary, or service-related, activities. Have you heard of the *postindustrial* or *information-based* economy? This is the economic activity to which those terms refer.

Tertiary activities involve businesses and other enterprises that provide some specialized service. For example, many people are engaged in wholesale or retail sales. People who deliver meat, produce, canned goods, and other items to your grocery store are contributing to the tertiary economy, as are the people who stock the shelves, prepare the ads and coupons that influence your shopping decisions, check you out, and bag your groceries. The store's manager, buyers, butchers, and pharmacists are as well. Today, millions of Americans and Canadians spend their workday at a computer. They and many others are involved in the changing economy based on the "information revolution." People who provide all of these services need to be educated, healthy, legally protected, and insured. Ensuring that these needs are met employs millions of skilled professionals.

TRADE AND COMMERCE

Families have needs that they are unable to meet themselves. They also provide something of worth—whether some material item or a service—for which they receive an income. Of course, there are always bills to pay for goods and services received. The United States and Canada manufacture many items and provide many services that are exported. They also have needs that cannot be met domestically. These items or services must be imported. All such exchanges involve selling and buying.

Economic Geography

Beer made for Canada's Mountain Crest Brewing Company rolls into the shipping area at Joseph Huber Brewing Company in Monroe, Wisconsin. The Canadian brewer's products are sold in Canada as well as in Wisconsin and other Midwestern states.

Not surprisingly, the United States and Canada are each other's major trading partner. In fact, these two countries do more business together than any other two countries in the world! Between 85 and 90 percent of all Canadian exports are destined for U.S. markets. Major items include automobiles and auto parts, wood pulp, and electricity. About 60 percent of Canada's imports, including many consumer goods and industrial supplies, also come from its neighbor. Nearly one-quarter of all U.S. exports and 15 to 20 percent of imports involve trade with Canada. In 1988, Canada and the United States signed the Canada-U.S. Free Trade Agreement (FTA). This economic dance, negotiated between the world's two greatest trading partners, was designed to remove high tariffs (fees) on goods traded between the two countries. In 1994, the agreement was expanded to include Mexico and became the North American Free Trade Agreement (NAFTA). So far, trade with Mexico has been rather limited.

The business relationship that exists between Northern America's neighboring countries is not without conflict. Canada, for example, can provide softwood (mostly for construction, newsprint, and wood pulp) to the United States for a lower price than that produced within the United States. To make up for the price difference, the United States government has imposed hefty duties (fees) on imported Canadian softwood. This added duty increases the price, so that consumers are more likely to purchase U.S. lumber. Canada has lost thousands of jobs because of this dispute, and the controversy has increased the cost of paper, homes, and other construction projects in the United States.

Other difficulties have also strained economic relations. In January 2003, a single cow in Alberta tested positive for mad cow disease. Canada's 4.1-billion-dollar beef export market immediately dropped to virtually zero because many countries imposed a ban on imported Canadian beef. The outbreak of severe acute respiratory syndrome (SARS) initially had a significant negative impact on tourism, particularly in Toronto. The two countries also argue over water resources (of which Canada has plenty and the United States is increasingly in need) and Pacific salmon. Overall, however, Canada and the United States are extremely dependent on one another economically as well as in many other ways.

ECONOMIC ISSUES

Overall, the economy of Northern America is the world's strongest and most stable. Unemployment remains relatively low, averaging 4 to 8 percent during the past decade. Inflation is in check. The United States, in particular, labors under a huge national debt and trade deficit. The country is about 7 trillion dollars in debt (about $23,500 per man, woman, and child). It also imports nearly 700 billion dollars' worth of goods and services more than it exports every year, and the gap is growing.

Both countries face the problem of an aging population. There are fewer workers, particularly for entry-level jobs, and more people are approaching their retirement years or are retired. Immigration can provide some relief in providing workers. In both countries, however, pension plans are being severely stressed. It will take foresight and political courage to solve these problems.

As jobs change from those that require mainly brawn (primary industries) to those dependent on brainpower, both countries face the challenge of better educating certain segments of their respective populations. It is important that all able citizens be able to compete successfully in the twenty-first century's complex global economy.

CHAPTER 8

Regions of Northern America

Regions exist at many scales and are based on many factors. For example, North America is a continental region, Northern America is a cultural region, and the United States and Canada are political regions. You may live in Canada's Prairie Provinces or the American Southwest. There are landform regions, climatic and ecosystem regions, economic regions, and many others. This book is one in a series based on culture regions. Within Northern America alone, there are many differences in the ways in which people live. Foods, houses, agricultural crops, how people make a living, and many other aspects of life vary greatly from place to place, as do languages and accents, religious beliefs, and political views. This chapter presents a brief overview of subregions within Northern America.

THE EASTERN CORE

A core region is defined by its importance. Historically, economically, and in terms of population, eastern Northern America has been and is now the most important region. The United States grew from coastal settlements that extended from Georgia to New England. Canada grew from its historical foothold in the St. Lawrence Valley. Here were the first farms, factories, and cities. Both the Canadian and U.S. capitals, Ottawa and Washington, D.C., are located in the cores of their countries, as are the countries' largest cities, Toronto (5 million) and New York (21 million), respectively. The region has been and continues to be the industrial, business, and financial heart of both countries.

The Atlantic Northeast includes the New England states and the neighboring Atlantic-facing provinces of eastern Canada. This region clings to four centuries of European history and tradition, resulting in a strong sense of regional identity. Much of the land is rugged and forest covered. There are few natural resources and little fertile soil. In this harsh environment, people have long turned to the sea for their livelihood. Coastal waters teem with lobsters and other marine life. The Grand Banks, off the coast of Newfoundland, was one of the world's richest fishing grounds. Today, however, the industry has suffered from overfishing. Families that for generations turned to the sea to make a living now must find some other source of income. A growing tourist industry, including winter skiers, has helped some areas. The recent discovery of offshore oil and natural gas deposits also holds considerable promise for future economic development. Today, however, the Atlantic Northeast lags behind other regions in terms of economic development and population growth.

The industrial core extends from the Atlantic Coast, between Boston and Washington, D.C., inland to the Mississippi River. In this region, many cities became associated with particular manufactured products: Detroit was the center of the

At the center of Washington, D.C., sits the Capitol, where the Senate and House of Representatives meet to make the laws that govern the nation. Flags are flown from the north wing of the Capitol when the Senate is in session and from the south wing when the House is in session.

automotive industry, just as Pittsburgh was with steel and Akron, Ohio, with tires. On the western edge of the region, Chicago grew as a major transportation and industrial hub. St. Louis, a port city on the Mississippi River, lay claim to being the "Gateway to the West." Toronto grew as Canada's leading industrial, commercial, and financial center, a position held by New York City in the United States. Portions of Illinois, Indiana, Ohio, and Iowa lie within the Cornbelt, one of the world's most productive agricultural regions.

The Southeastern United States was an economically depressed region, dependent on agriculture and human labor for a long time. During the past 50 years, however, tremendous changes have occurred in the region's political, social, and economic landscape. Today, the South is progressive and prospering. Agriculture continues to be important, but it has been replaced by industry, services, and tourism as the chief sources of income. Atlanta, Georgia, has boomed during recent decades and become the region's major urban center. Orlando, Florida, with Disney World and other attractions, has become one of the country's leading tourist destinations.

Canada's core area centers on the St. Lawrence Valley and Great Lakes and the provinces of Quebec and Ontario. Here, early French and British settlers established towns. Along the St. Lawrence, the city of Quebec, steeped in Old World charm, stands as a sentinel above the river. Upstream, Montreal has boomed as Quebec's leading industrial and commercial center. It is Canada's second-largest city, with a metropolitan area population of 3.6 million. It is also the world's second-largest French-speaking city.

To the west is southern Ontario, home to 12 million people, roughly one-third of Canada's total population, and the country's economic hearth. Ontario means "sparkling" or "beautiful water" in the Iroquois language. The province faces four of the Great Lakes and extends northward to Hudson Bay. To many Canadians, the region's natural essence is captured by views of lakes on misty mornings and the chants of loons floating over their glassy surfaces. Ontario's economy was built on natural resources such as fur, minerals, and timber. Today, southern Ontario is a magnet for manufacturing and service industries, science, and the arts.

"Change" may be the word that best describes the Eastern core today. Smoke-belching factories surrounded by dreary residential areas are largely a thing of the past. Today, downtown banks and other businesses create an urban skyline of prosperity. In many areas, suburban areas teem with gleaming buildings that house postindustrial businesses: services, information-based industries, and corporate headquarters.

After decades of decline, the "Rustbelt" is beginning to show signs of revival. As is true throughout most of Northern America, huge malls, supermarkets, chain hotels and motels, and other corporate enterprises long ago replaced most small family-owned-and-operated businesses.

THE SPACIOUS HEARTLAND

The "heartland" is a difficult region to define. Here, it is identified as the interior of the continent—a vast area that extends from roughly the Mississippi River westward across the Great Plains and includes the mountains, basins, and plateaus of the interior West. In a north-south direction, the heartland extends from the Gulf of Mexico to the Arctic shores. It is a region characterized by somewhat harsh and challenging environmental conditions, a low population density, and dependence on primary industries. For nearly a century, much of the region has experienced economic-decline and outmigration, leaving small rural settlements to wither away.

In both Canada and the United States, the heartland was the last settlement frontier. Throughout the entire area, few communities were settled before the second half of the nineteenth century. The primary exceptions are some native settlements (several Southwestern Native American pueblos date to the mid-eleventh century), Spanish-settled communities in the Southwest, and lands that surround the western Great Lakes.

Economically, the region can be divided into several zones defined—although not well—by the primary industry. From the wetter east to drier west, they are mixed crop agriculture and livestock; livestock ranching and irrigated agriculture; and mining, logging, and tourism. East of the 100th meridian, which passess roughly through the center of the U.S. and Canada, enough moisture falls to allow the growing of most crops without irrigation. Corn, small grains, soybeans, hay, and other crops thrive throughout the region. In the Great Plains, hardy grains such as wheat and grain sorghum are raised on huge farms that often cover thousands of acres. In the Southwest, cotton is a major crop in a band that stretches from Texas to southern Arizona. Livestock ranching is also a major activity, here, particularly on the drier western margins, where most crops can be grown only with irrigation.

Farther west, rugged terrain limits agriculture and access. Here, from Arizona northward into Canada, mineral resources proved to be the primary magnet for early settlement and economic activity. In Texas and Oklahoma and, more recently, Alberta and northern Alaska, petroleum fueled development. Throughout the mountainous West, settlers were lured first by rich deposits of gold and silver and then by copper and other nonprecious minerals. Today, much of the Western landscape is dotted with abandoned mining operations, tailings (residue) dumps, and ghost towns. The vast north, although inhabited by various native groups, remained a remote frontier to European settlers.

On the western plains, Denver, the "Mile High City," thrives as a regional trade center, as do Winnipeg, Manitoba, and Calgary, Alberta, in Canada. Farther north in Alberta is Edmonton, one of the great surprises of Northern America. Here, at 53 degrees north latitude, is a city of nearly one million people that is home to the world's largest shopping mall! In the West Edmonton Mall, in addition to shopping and dining, one can ride a roller coaster or submarine, bungee jump or surf (on the world's largest indoor lake), or ice skate.

Many areas within the heartland are now undergoing great change. Some areas, particularly small communities, are experiencing rapid decline. Larger regional centers, however, are growing, particularly those in the Sunbelt. Houston, Dallas, and Oklahoma City are large metropolitan centers with diverse and thriving economies, as are Albuquerque, Phoenix, and Tucson.

The World Waterpark at West Edmonton Mall contains the world's largest indoor wave pool. There are 23 slides and attractions within the waterpark. The highest slides are 85 feet (26 meters).

Las Vegas, of course, has exploded in population as a tourist destination because of its casinos. People are attracted to the Southwest's dry climate, sunshine, and opportunities to pursue outdoor recreational activities, such as golf, all year. Air-conditioning makes comfortable year-round living possible. Water is drawn from wells hundreds of feet deep or diverted from streams often hundreds of miles distant. Culture and technology have combined to make this the fastest-growing region of Northern America.

In the mountainous interior, many of the old mining communities are now thriving tourist centers, often built around ski resorts. After decades of decline, many areas in the rugged western interior are once again thriving. The region offers many spectacular landscapes, a fascinating frontier history, numerous native cultures, and countless recreational opportunities. From Arizona to Alaska, tourism is booming. The area also is drawing a great number of retirees who boost local populations and economies.

THE BOOMING WEST COAST

The Pacific Coast, which includes Alaska and Hawaii, has led Northern America in population and economic growth during the past half-century. Because of the rugged nature of the land—it is sandwiched between towering mountains and the sea—the region is dominated by cities. From south to north, San Diego, Los Angeles, and San Francisco form a huge conurbation (continuous urban area), "San-San," that has a population of nearly 30 million. California long ago became the first ranking state in population, agriculture, manufacturing, trade and commerce, services, the entertainment industry, and tourism. To the north, Portland, Oregon, and Seattle, Washington, are thriving urban centers, as is Vancouver, British Columbia. These cities are growing rapidly both in population and in economic importance. Many visitors also would agree that they are among Northern America's most attractive cities. Anchorage, Alaska, and Honolulu, Hawaii, although not huge, have shared in the region's growth.

Initially, the West Coast economy was based on primary industries. Gold attracted early fortune seekers to the California gold fields and later to British Columbia and Alaska. Fishing was once of great importance throughout the region. Although the industry is in decline, it is of major importance in British Columbia and Alaska. Logging has long been a major activity from northern California northward into Alaska's panhandle. Today, because of stricter environmental laws—such as those that protect the endangered spotted owl—this industry has

The Napa Valley in California is only 30 miles (48 kilometers) long but contains well over 200 wineries. Most of the wineries offer tours and tasting rooms for visitors.

suffered, as have the people and communities that depended on logging and related industries. Although limited in its extent, agriculture, too, is important in many areas of the West Coast. California's Central Valley is the leading agricultural area of the United States. To the north, in Oregon's Willamette Valley, nearly 70 different cash crops are raised. Throughout the region, many specialty crops that bring a high value are grown. A Great Plains wheat farmer, for example, may profit $25 per acre in a good year. An acre of Napa Valley grapes, in comparison, may produce $25,000 or more in vintage wine.

For decades, California has been the primary center of Northern America's ever-changing popular culture. The media industry—motion pictures, music, television, radio, and print media—in particular, has influenced fads and trends throughout the region and the world. Today, it still is a center of culture change. With the possible exception of New York City, the West Coast has always been Northern America's region of greatest cultural and ethnic diversity. San Francisco and Vancouver are famous for their tolerance and openness to cultural change. As documented by the 2000 census, people of northwestern European culture are now in the minority in California. California's non-Anglo population is dominantly Latino and Asian; elsewhere in the western region, people from various East Asian countries dominate the ethnic landscape.

Much like a kaleidoscope, Northern America's regions will continue to change. Some areas will grow, others will decline. Economic activities will change, as will population and settlement. Certainly, culture and ethnicity will continue to diversify as an increasing number of people are attracted to this prosperous region of expanding opportunity.

CHAPTER 9

Northern America Looks Ahead

As anyone who depends on weather reports knows, forecasting future events can be difficult and the results are not always accurate. Geographer Erhard Rostlund noted that "the present is the fruit of the past and contains the seeds of the future." Simply stated, if a person looks first to the past and observes trends that led to present conditions, the task of looking ahead is made simpler and forecasts are more apt to be accurate. Using historical geography, past trends, and present-day conditions as their guide, the authors will attempt paint a picture of Northern America's future.

Changes within the physical environment usually occur slowly. Mountains grow and erode, continents drift, and water bodies come and go, as do ice ages. Such changes occur at a pace measured by geologic time, over thousands or even millions of years. Some changes—such as earthquakes, tsunamis, volcanic eruptions, and earth slides—occur rapidly and with greater frequency. The same is true of tornadoes, hurricanes, floods, and droughts. Every year, fires ravage woodlands and grasslands. Nature is always restless, and each of these events will continue to occur.

Data suggest that the global climate is warming. In terms of temperature, precipitation, drought, and other weather-related events, the potential outcome remains unclear. It seems certain, however, that a warmer climate will bring many changes throughout Northern America. Much of Canada and Alaska is underlain by permafrost. Warming conditions will cause ground frozen beneath the surface to thaw, which, in turn, will result in catastrophic damage. Buildings, highways, railroads, and other structures will be affected as their foundation of frozen ground begins to turn to earthen mush. With a warming climate, hurricanes are becoming more numerous and intense. As temperatures warm and some places become drier and others wetter, ecosystems will change. This will cause a migration of many species of plants and animals. Others will become extinct because of their inability to adapt to rapidly changing environmental conditions.

Certainly, the thirst for water used in irrigation, industry, and home consumption will increase. Providing adequate supplies of this essential resource will become increasing costly and challenging. This is particularly true for water-starved areas such as California and the desert Southwest. Today, rivers such as the Colorado and Rio Grande often are dry long before their channels reach their mouths. Few areas in the United States have an adequate supply of clean water. The future almost certainly will bring massive water diversion projects from areas of plenty to places of need. Canada has abundant fresh water resources, which, ultimately, may be diverted southward. Currently, however, many details must be worked out between the two countries if this is to happen.

A logger measures fallen trees at a tree farm in Washington State. The term *tree farming* was first used in the 1940s. It implies commitment to the land and was the philosophical opposite of the "cut-out and get-out" philosophy of the early twentieth century.

Timber is a vital and renewable resource. Increasingly, in both the United States and Canada, there is widespread recognition that conservation measures must be implemented in such a way as to ensure the future availability of wood, pulp, and paper. In fact, today, much of our wood comes from tree "farms." Fortunately, soils are being used much more wisely than they were even half a century ago. Today, new tillage practices, terracing, and other measures are greatly reducing soil erosion.

Natural disasters will continue to occur, and their toll undoubtedly will increase. Natural disasters can best be defined as people and their built environment being out of place; people place themselves at risk by living and building in hazardous zones. This is true of cities located on fault zones, such as Los Angeles and San Francisco. There are many communities in low-lying hurricane prone coastal regions, such as Miami and recently devastated New Orleans (much of which is actually below sea level!). In the West, many settlements are in areas subject to frequent raging forest fires; others are built on top of or at the base of unstable land that can break away as an avalanche or earth flow. There are many other examples of people taking environmental risks. Sadly, as more people choose to place themselves in jeopardy, nature's toll of destruction undoubtedly will increase.

During the coming decades, many changes in population will occur. Both countries are experiencing a sharp decline in their rate of natural population increase. Populations in both countries continue to grow, primarily as a result of immigration. This suggests that Northern America's economic health surely will become increasingly dependent on immigrants. Immigration policies, therefore, must be cautious yet flexible. Future employment needs must be thoughtfully considered. Of particular concern will be the need for laborers to offset an aging society that places strain on retirement programs and other needs.

Major changes also can be anticipated in settlement. Many cities, particularly in the United States, are decaying. It remains to be seen whether current efforts at inner-city renewal will bear fruit. Planner Kyle Ezell, a cultural geographer, believes that inner-city revitalization will change the urban landscape much as the growth of suburbs did during the twentieth century. Others believe that the growth of megacities will stall during coming decades. As jobs become less tied to place, many people may choose to live in places where the pace of life is slower and less stressful. Because these people are accustomed to the things that cities can offer, this will particularly favor middle-size communities. Attractive rural areas, such as Appalachia, the Ozarks, and western mountain areas will continue to grow in importance. Even Canada's chilly interior and beautiful eastern Maritime Provinces may begin to attract new settlers if access and economic opportunity improve.

Culture and society certainly will change at a fast pace during coming decades. Northern America will become increasingly multicultural. In many areas, including California, people of Anglo-European origin already are in a minority, and that trend will continue. A culturally diverse society offers many benefits. Diversity can also create problems, however. It is essential that all peoples are respected and have an equal opportunity to partake of the bounty offered by the region's way of life. For this to occur, all groups must be able to compete on an equal footing. The best way to ensure widespread social integration and economic success is through education, which must be a top priority. Also important are the ability to communicate with one another and a set of shared values.

Both the United States and Canada have a long history of good government. People, it can be said, have the government that they deserve, and there are troubling signs on the political landscape. Political parties and many politicians seem more concerned with their own advancement than they are in serving the public that elected them to office. Many citizens are becoming increasingly polarized and extreme in their views. Many also are woefully ignorant of the issues. They either fail to vote or cast votes based on political party affiliation rather than on the merit of candidates' views on issues themselves. Much political debate has become little more than a mudslinging contest. Rarely are issues debated in depth or thoughtfully explained. Many people feel that elected officials are influenced more by lobbyists than by their constituents' wishes. Northern America's political systems may be among the world's best, but they cannot be taken for granted. Some major changes must be implemented if the blessing of good government is to last.

Canada's political future remains in doubt. The country is more geographically and ideologically fragmented than the

United States. Each of Canada's provinces has its own political agenda, to a much greater extent than U.S. states do. French Quebec stands apart from all other provinces. The resource-rich and somewhat conservative Prairie Provinces rarely see eye to eye on issues with more liberal British Columbia or Ontario. Fortunately, however, there are signs that, as a country, Canada is successfully resolving many of these issues and is beginning to pull together, rather than splintering.

Economically, Northern America also is approaching a crossroads. Increasingly, the region faces stern economic competition from China, Japan, India, the European Union, and elsewhere. Competition is particularly keen for natural resources (particularly petroleum) and expanding markets. Population giants China and India are rising rapidly as both energy consumers and industrial giants. Canada and the United States must adjust to these global changes. No longer can they compete on the global stage with blue-collar labor and smoke-belching factories. The region must continue to move swiftly toward leadership in a postindustrial economy that features information, services, and global networking. This will require a well-governed and highly educated population. It will also depend on a society that is geographically literate. To compete successfully today, one must possess a global "mental map" with detailed images of the world's cultures, places, conflicts, needs, and linkages.

Regions will also experience change. Northern Americans have often moved as regional conditions and opportunities change. Both Canada and the United States have huge areas of relatively vacant land. Might Canada's northern interior and Maritime Provinces, as well as the Great Plains in both countries, be the next areas of economic boom and resulting population growth? Will people continue to be attracted to the Sunbelt as the region becomes increasingly crowded and costly? What effect might a sharp increase in the cost of energy, resulting in spiraling heating and cooling bills, have on migration and settlement? Fifty years ago, few would have predicted the tremendous population growth in the hot, arid, American Southwest. Massive water projects and the development of effective air-conditioning, however, contributed to spectacular growth. Who could have predicted a doubling of Alaska's population over a 30-year period, largely as a result of tapping the state's petroleum resources? Since the 1960s, the U.S. South has undergone tremendous change, largely as a result of civil rights legislation and racial integration. What will result from immigration? Specific changes are difficult to forecast. The authors can predict, however, that the regional map of Northern America look much different 50 years from now.

As you have seen, Northern America has been blessed in countless ways. It is a region rich in environmental diversity, vast space, and a wealth of natural resources. It also is blessed with a boundless gift of diverse human resources. Perhaps the insight contained in Rostlund's statement gives us the best glimpse of the future: Northern America's past has produced an abundance of fine fruit, and this fruit, almost certainly, has sown the seeds of a very positive future.

HISTORY AT A GLANCE

Before 12000 B.C.	Ice Age glaciers begin to recede; earliest evidence places humans in Northern America.
9000 B.C.	Most of Northern America is inhabited by native peoples.
A.D. 1003	Vikings establish a settlement at Hop (L'Anse aux Meadows) in northern Newfoundland.
1497	Giovanni Caboto (John Cabot) is the first European explorer to reach the shores of Northern America.
1507	The name "America" first appears on a map.
1540	Coronado leads a band of Spanish explorers into present-day New Mexico and as far as present-day Kansas.
1547	Maps begin to call the land north of the St. Lawrence River "Canada."
1565	Spaniards establish St. Augustine (Florida), which becomes the first permanent settled European community in Northern America.
1605	The French settle Annapolis (Nova Scotia).
1607	The British settle at Jamestown (Virginia).
1608	Samuel de Champlain establishes the settlement of Quebec on the St. Lawrence River.
1610	Henry Hudson explores the bay that later bears his name; the Spanish settle Santa Fe (New Mexico).
1670	The Hudson's Bay Company is founded.
1776	The American Revolution begins; America gains independence on July 4.
1793	Alexander Mackenzie crosses Canada to reach the Pacific Coast.
1803	The United States buys the Louisiana Territory from France for 15 million dollars, expanding its territory by 800,000 square miles (2 million square kilometers).
1804	President Thomas Jefferson sends the Corps of Discovery, an expedition headed by Lewis and Clark, to explore the west to the shores of the Pacific Ocean; the exploration lasts two years.
1841	The Province of Canada is formed from Upper and Lower Canada.
1848	Gold is discovered at Sutter's Mill, east of San Francisco, California, resulting in the massive gold rush of 1849.

HISTORY AT A GLANCE

1861–1865	The Civil War bitterly divides the United States, pitting the slave-holding Southern states against the North.
1863	The Emancipation Proclamation frees slaves in the United States.
1867	The British North American Act establishes the Dominion of Canada; Alaska is purchased from Russia for 7.2 million dollars.
1869	The United States completes the first transcontinental railway.
1885	Canada's transcontinental railroad is completed.
1897	The Klondike gold rush begins.
1900	The Galveston (Texas) hurricane kills as many as 8,000 people in Northern America's greatest natural disaster as measured by loss of life.
1906	A San Francisco earthquake kills 500 and nearly destroys the city.
1929	The Great Depression begins, bringing financial ruin to millions.
1930s	Much of interior Northern America suffers severe drought, resulting in "Dust Bowl" conditions; thousands of displaced people migrate to California, beginning the state's population boom.
1939–1945	Canada and United States are involved in World War II.
1959	Alaska and Hawaii become the forty-ninth and fiftieth U.S. states, respectively, and the United States's current flag is adopted.
1964	Alaska experiences a 9.2 magnitude earthquake, perhaps the strongest quake ever recorded, resulting in more than 130 deaths.
1965	Canada adopts a new flag.
1980	Mount St. Helens (Washington) erupts violently, killing 57 people and destroying an area of several thousand square miles.
1989	The Canada–U.S. Free Trade Agreement (FTA) is signed.
1992	Hurricane Andrew strikes Florida and Louisiana, resulting in a then-record 25 billion dollars in property losses.
1994	The FTA is re-signed as the North American Free Trade Agreement (NAFTA); it includes Mexico and spurs trade among the three countries.
1995	A Quebec government referendum on secession fails by a narrow margin.

HISTORY AT A GLANCE

2001 On September 11, terrorists hijack four commercial flights and attack the Twin Towers of the World Trade Center in New York City and the Pentagon in Washington, D.C.; an estimated 3,000 lives are lost.

2005 Hurricane Katrina strikes the Gulf Coast, resulting in 1,200 deaths and 200 billion dollars in property losses from Louisiana to Alabama.

FURTHER READING

Atlas of the United States of America. Washington, D.C.: United States Department of the Interior–U. S. Geological Survey, 1970.

Birdsall, Stephen S., John W. Florin, and Margo L. Price. *Regional Landscapes of the United States and Canada.* New York: John Wiley & Sons, 1999.

Boal, Frederick W., and Stephen A. Royle, eds. *North America: A Geographical Mosaic.* London: Arnold, 1999.

Desaulniers, Kristi L. *Canada.* Philadelphia: Chelsea House Publishers, 2003.

Garreau, Joel. *The Nine Nations of North America.* Boston: Houghton Mifflin Company, 1981.

Garrett, Wilbur E., ed. *Atlas of North America.* Washington, D.C.: National Geographic Society, 1985.

Garrett, Wilbur E., ed. *Historical Atlas of the United States.* Washington, D.C.: National Geographic Society, 1988.

Grabowski, John F. *Canada.* San Diego, CA: Lucent Books, 1998.

Hakim, Joy. *The First Americans, Prehistory–1608.* New York: Oxford University Press, 2003.

King, David C. *Smithsonian Children's Encyclopedia of American History.* New York: DK Publishing, 2003.

McKnight, Tom L. *Regional Geography of the United States and Canada,* 4th edition. Upper Saddle River, NJ: Pearson Education, Inc., 2004.

McNeese, Tim. *The Mississippi River.* Philadelphia: Chelsea House Publishers, 2004.

McNeese, Tim. *The St. Lawrence River.* Philadelphia: Chelsea House Publishers, 2005.

The National Atlas of Canada. Toronto: Macmillan, 1974.

Pang, Guek-Cheng. *Cultures of the World, Canada.* New York: Marshall Cavendish International—Benchmark Books, 2004.

Rogers, Barbara Radcliffe, and Stillman D. Rogers. *Canada, Enchantment of the World.* New York: Children's Press, 2000.

FURTHER READING

Rooney, John F., Jr., Wilbur Zelinsky, and Dean R. Louder, eds. *This Remarkable Continent: An Atlas of United States and Canadian Society and Cultures.* College Station, TX: Texas A&M University Press, 1982.

Smolan, Rick, ed. *A Day in the Life of Canada.* Don Mills, Ontario: Collins Publishers, 1984.

NOTE: For further and current information on the United States or Canada, any of their political subunits, or specific topics such as the environment, population, and economic, political, social, or other data, please use Internet search engines as appropriate. An excellent general information source for any of the world's countries is the CIA factbook at www.cia.gov/cia/publications/factbook (Canada; United States).

INDEX

Acadia, 49. *See also* Nova Scotia
Africans, 39, 51
agriculture, 20. *See also* farming; plantations
   in Canada/U.S., 42, 96–97
   as primary industry, 86–88
   settlement, water and, 24–26, 56
   soils and, 10, 14, 42
   on West Coast, 101–102
   westward expansion and, 42, 56
air-conditioners, 60, 99, 110
aircraft industry, 90
air traffic, 80
Alaska, 10, 28, 74–75, 78, 110
amenity locations, 61
Anasazi cliff dwellings, 33
Anglo America, 2–3
animals, 20, 71, 78, 101. *See also* specific animals
Appalachian Mountains, 13, 40, 61, 107–108
aqueducts, 55
architecture, 70, 71
Asians, 3, 31, 43, 51, 61, 103. *See also* Chinese people; Japan
Atlantic and Gulf Coastal Plains, 12–13
Australia, 5, 45
automobiles, 53, 56–57, 90, 95–96
avalanches, 26–27, 107

basins, 12, 14, 23
   interior plateaus and, 15–17
Bay of Fundy, 11
beer, 91
Beringia (Bering Strait "land bridge"), 31
bison, 20–21, 34
blacks, 61
blizzards, 26
Bonneville Salt Flats, 16
Britain, 3, 36–40, 49, 72, 76
Buddhism, 69
buffalo. *See* bison
Buffalo Bill, 21

bull, changing of history by, 35–36
Bush, George W., 77
businesses, 80, 82, 83
Bytown, 58. *See also* Ottawa

Cabot, John, 36
California
   climate of, 22
   as economic power, 81–82, 101
   gold rush, 40, 52, 101
   Gulf of, 25
   Los Angeles, 28, 59, 101, 107
   population of, 26, 43, 55, 108
   San Francisco, 28, 101, 103, 107
   water and, 26, 55, 105
Canada. *See also* specific cities/regions
   agriculture in U.S. v., 42, 96–97
   area/sq. miles of, 44
   Britain and, 72, 76
   cities in U.S. and, 59–60, 95–103
   culture of U.S. v., 1–2, 8, 31
   eastern core of, 95–97
   English language in, 2, 8, 43, 65, 78
   flags of, 64, 66
   French language/people in, 2, 3, 8, 38, 43, 65, 72, 78, 109
   gold rush, 52
   governments of U.S. v., 60, 76–78, 108–109
   heartland region of, 98–101
   Maritime Provinces, 62, 78, 108, 109
   minorities in, 2, 61, 103
   nation building and, 74–76
   politics and, 43, 94, 108–109
   population of U.S. v., 44–48
   ports in, 55
   safety of, 29
   separatism in, 65–67
   taxes in U.S. v., 60
   tidal range in, 11
   trade between U.S. and, 91–92
   travel between U.S. and, 2
   U.S. border with, 52, 72
   Vikings and, 35–36

INDEX

water, U.S. and, 92, 105
westward expansion and, 42, 51–53, 74–76
Canadian Rockies, 15
Canadian shield, 14
canals, 23, 25, 40
canyons, 15, 16
Cartier, Jacques, 37
Catholicism, 5, 49, 68
census data, 45, 47, 103
Champlain, Samuel de, 38
China, 109
Chinese people, 42, 51
Christianity, 68–69
cities. *See also specific cities*
   cultural change in, 70
   in eastern core, 95–97
   in heartland, 99–100
   settlement and, 57–62
   in U.S. and Canada, 59–60, 95–103
   on West Coast, 101, 103
civil rights legislation, 110
climates, 10, 11, 18. *See also* global warming
   ecosystems and, 18–22, 83, 94
   zones, 19
clothing, 35, 71, 89
Clovis site, 31
coal, 83, 89
coastal indentations, 12–13, 17
coasts. *See also* Pacific Coast; West Coast region
   population on, 45–47, 54
   ranges, 17–18
   settlements on, 53, 95
   shipping and, 53
colonies, 31, 37–40, 43, 49, 75
Colorado Rockies, 24
Columbus, Christopher, 32, 36
commerce, 57, 59, 90–92
communication, instant, 86
computers, 70–71, 85, 86, 90
confederation, 74
Congress, 77
conservation, 106

constitutions, 76, 78
continents, 3, 5, 94, 104
conurbation (continuous urban area), 101
Cornbelt, 96
courts, 78
cows, diseased, 92
crops, 83, 98–99
cultural change, 70, 103
cultural ecology, 11
cultural history, 36–40
cultural relativity, change and, 70–71
cultures, 2. *See also* native cultures
   adaptation by, 9, 11
   assimilation of, 6–7, 43
   of Canada v. U.S., 1–2, 8, 31
   common threads defining, 30
   development and diffusion of, 70–71
   diversity of, 1, 43, 61–62, 103, 108
   economic growth and, 84–86
   folk, 7, 59
   indigenous, 6, 65–67, 72
   native, 32–35
   nature and, 11
   popular, 7–8, 13, 59, 71–72, 102–103
   regions, 1–9, 2–5, 63, 94
   settlement patterns and, 58–61
   society and, 63–72
   symbols of, 63–69
   technology and, 54, 70–71

dams, 12, 15–16, 23, 25, 80
Death Valley, 17, 21–22
democracy, 5, 43, 70, 76
demographics, 45, 47
deserts, 10, 24–25
development
   climate's impact on, 18
   diffusion of culture and, 70–71
   economic, 6, 10, 25–26, 45, 62, 79–80, 82–86
   tourism and, 17
diet, food and, 69, 71
droughts, 22, 26, 105

INDEX

Dust Bowl, 42
Dutch settlers, 38, 49

earthquakes, 26, 28, 105
earth slides, 105, 107
eastern core region, 95–98
economic activities, 86–90, 103
economic development
    foundations of, 82–86
    government and, 80
    settlement and, 6, 10, 45, 62, 79
    water and, 25–26
economic geography, 81–93
economic issues, 92–93
economic stability, 85
economy
    "boom and bust," 17
    competition with, 109
    of eastern core, 95–98
    folk/popular culture and, 59
    government and, 80, 82
    growth of, cultural contributors to, 84–86
    of heartland, 98–101
    information and, 48, 61, 90, 109
    market, 5, 43, 70, 80, 82, 85
    measures of, 48
    postindustrial/information-based, 61, 90, 109
    settlement and, 54, 62
    of West Coast region, 101–102
ecosystems, 10
    climates and, 18–22, 83, 94
    culture's impact on, 9
    diversity in, 11
Edmonton Mall, West, 100
education, 44, 48, 86, 93, 109
Ellis Island, 52
energy, 80, 89, 109. *See also* hydroelectric power
English language, 3, 5, 65, 67
    in Canada, 2, 8, 43, 65, 78
environment
    changes in, 104–105
    natural, 83–84, 86

environmental hazards, 26–29
environmental laws, 80, 101
environmental restrictions, 86, 88
E pluribus unum (from many, one), 6–7
erosion, 6, 15, 106
Eskimos. *See* Inuit
Europe, 2
    colonization by, 31, 37–40, 43, 49
    exploration by, 31, 32, 36–39
    immigration and, 31, 40–43, 48–51, 65
    Native Americans impacted by, 6, 36, 40, 49
    Northern America impacted by, 3, 5–6, 8, 31–32, 35–43, 65, 70–71, 95
    population in, 45, 47
    religion and, 67, 70
    settlement and, 31, 37–40, 48–51
European Union, 109
exports, 71–72, 90–93
Ezell, Kyle, 107

factories, 83, 97
fall line, 13
farming. *See also* crops
    fish, 88
    government and, 80
    by native cultures, 33–34
    on Pacific Coast, 17
    on plains, 12, 83
    in Quebec, 84
    railroads and, 56–57
    ranching and, 88
    reverting to woodland, 20
    soil fertility and, 55–56, 88
    tree, 106
fault zones, 28, 29, 107
fertility rate, 47
fires, 29, 105, 107
First Americans, 31–32
First Nations, 32
    Cree, 65

118

INDEX

fishing, 26
   Britain and, 49
   economy and, 83, 86, 88
   Grand Banks, 36, 49, 88, 95
   settlement and, 57
   on West Coast, 101
fjords, 18
flags, 63–64, 66, 68, 96
floods, 15–16, 26–28, 105
Florida, 39, 49, 50, 97
folk culture, 7, 59
food
   diet and, 69, 71
   production, 88
forests, 6, 20, 22, 107. *See also* logging; taiga; trees
Fort, in community names, 57–58
fossil fuels, 11
"Four Corners" area, 15
France
   exploration/colonization by, 37–40, 49
   land survey system, 79
freedoms
   individual/personal, 7, 43, 71, 78
   to worship, 67–69
Free Trade Agreement (FTA), 91–92
French Canadians, 2, 3, 8, 38, 43, 65, 72, 78, 109
FTA. *See* Free Trade Agreement
fur trade, 36–37, 39, 49

Gadsden Purchase, 75
gaps, 13
GDP. *See* gross domestic product
geography, 20
   economic, 81–93
   historical, 30–43
   political, 73–80
German settlers, 38, 40, 50–51, 65
glaciers, 14, 15, 18, 23, 31
globalization, 72
global markets/economy, 82, 85–86, 93, 109

global warming, 105
gold, 37, 49, 84, 99
   rush, 40, 52, 101
governments, 9, 48
   of Canada v. U.S., 60, 76–78, 108–109
   capitals, 58, 95
   criticizing, 78
   economy and, 80, 82
   Executive/Legislative/Judical branches of, 76–78
   good, 73, 108
   land, resources and, 78–80
   political geography and, 73–80
   self-, 67, 76
   taxes and, 60, 80
grains, 14, 20, 99. *See also* Marquis wheat
Grand Banks, Newfoundland, 36, 49, 88, 95
Grand Canyon, 15, 16
grasslands, 20
Great Depression, 25, 42
Great Lakes, 14, 23–24, 37, 54
   lowlands, 14
Great Plains, 14, 29, 99, 109
Great Salt Lake, 16
Greeley, Horace, 51
gross domestic product (GDP), 81
groundwater, 23
Gulf of California, 25
Gulf of Mexico, 12, 27, 37, 98
Gulf of St. Lawrence, 12, 36

hail, 26
harbors, natural, 12–13, 17, 26
Hawaii, 10, 18, 22, 75, 78
hazards
   environmental, 26–29
   natural, 11
   zones, 29, 107
health, 47–48, 74
heartland region, 98–101
Hell's Canyon, 15
Henry VII (king of England), 36

119

INDEX

highways, 54, 56–57
  economy and, 83, 85
  government and, 80
  roads and, 57, 74
Hinduism, 69
Hispanics, 3, 39, 43, 61, 72
historical geography, 30–43
history
  bull's changing of, 35–36
  conflicts in, 1
  cultural, 36–40
Homestead Act, 56
House of Commons, 76–77
House of Representatives, 77, 96
humans
  impacts of, 11, 20, 24–26
  land use by, 10, 12, 17, 20
  as resources, 45, 48, 82, 110
  risk, natural disasters and, 29, 107
  water use by, 25–26
hurricanes, 26–29, 105
hydroelectric power, 14, 25, 26, 80

ice
  ages, 14, 15, 23, 31–32, 104
  dams, 15–16
  freezing, 26
  Inuit words for snow and, 66
  sheets, continental, 23
immigration, 110. *See also* migration
  by Europeans, 31, 40–43, 48–51, 65
  jobs and, 93
  legal/illegal, 43, 47
  population and, 47, 107
  railroads and, 41–42
  settlement and, 61–62
imports, exports and, 90–93
India, 109
Indians, 32, 32–34, 79. *See also* Native Americans
indigenous cultures, 6, 65–67, 72
Industrial and Commercial Revolutions, 85
industrial core, 95–97

industries. *See also* specific industries
  building, 83, 89
  environmental restrictions on, 86, 88
  extractive, 83, 86–89
  government and, 78, 80
  lumber, 78, 92
  primary, 84, 86–89, 93, 98–99, 101–102
  secondary, 89–90
  settlement patterns and, 59, 61
  tertiary, 90
  urbanization and, 5, 42
inflation, 92
information, 7, 48, 61, 90, 109
integration, 108, 110
interior lowland plains, 14
interior plateaus and basins, 15–17
Internet, 85
Inuit (Eskimo), 34–35, 40, 65–67, 70
Ireland, 50
Islam, 69
islands, 12–13, 18, 52. *See also* Hawaii
Italy, 51

Jamestown, Virginia, 38
Japan, 47, 109
jobs. *See also* retirement
  aging population and, 47–48, 93
  economy and, 86–93
  education and, 86, 93
  immigration and, 93
  outsourcing, 85–86
  settlement and, 47, 54, 58–61
John Paul II, 68
Judaism, 69

Karlsefni, Thorfinn, 35–36

lakes, 10, 23
  canals and, 23
  Great Lakes, 14, 23–24, 37, 54
  Great Salt, 16
  locks and, 23–24
  Mead, 25
  Missoula, 15

INDEX

Powell, 25
ships on, 23–24
Superior, 23
Winnipeg, 89
land features, 10, 11. *See also specific features*
names of, 35
patterns for, 12
lands. *See also* lowlands; scablands; woodlands
government, resources and, 78–80
Indian trust, 79
public, 74, 78–79
purchasing, 79
survey systems, 74, 79
land use, 5, 12
government control of, 80
by humans, 10, 12, 17, 20
map, 87
languages
diversity, and stability in U.S., 67
English, 2, 3, 5, 8, 43, 65, 67, 78
French, 2, 3, 8, 38, 43, 65, 72, 78, 109
Inuit, 65–66
Iroquois, 97
Spanish, 67
as symbols, 63, 64–67
L'Anse aux Meadows, Newfoundland, 35–36
Latin America, 2–3, 36–37
Latinos, 103
latitudes, 18
laws, 7, 74, 80, 101
less-developed countries (LDCs), 70
life expectancies, 44, 47–48
life quality, 44
literacy, education and, 44, 48
livestock, 14, 20–21, 83, 99
locations, 53–58, 61
locks, 23–24, 25
logging, 22, 106. *See also* lumber industry
Britain and, 49
economy and, 83, 86–87, 89

settlement and, 57, 58
on West Coast, 101
Louisiana Purchase, 75
lowlands, 12
Great Lakes, 14
lumber industry, 78, 92. *See also* mills

Macdonald, Sir John A., 42
Macy's Thanksgiving Day parade, 8
manufacturing, 84–87, 89–90, 95–97
maple sugar, 64
Marquis wheat, 42
Martin, Paul, 77
McPherson, Helen Gordon, 72
media, 71–72, 102–103
melting pot, 1, 51
metals, 84, 89
Mexico, 39
Cession of 1846, 75
Gulf of, 12, 27, 37, 98
trade with, 92
migration, 7
of First Americans, 31–32
natural resources and, 6
property values and, 29, 61
settlement and, 50–53, 109–110
westward expansion and, 51–53
military, 74
mills, 13, 26
mineral resources, 6, 11, 57, 83–84
in Canadian shield, 14
extraction of, 88–89
gold, 37, 40, 49, 52, 84, 99, 101
silver, 37, 84, 99
mining, 55, 100
in Canadian shield, 14
economy and, 17, 86, 88–89
ghost towns, 61, 99
minorities, 2, 3, 61, 72, 103, 108. *See also specific minorities*
mobility, 7
Montreal, 41, 55, 59, 97
mountains, 12, 83. *See also* ranges
Appalachian, 13, 40, 61, 107–108
basins separating, 16–17

121

INDEX

changes in, 104
climate impacted by, 21–22
Denali, 18
Logan, 18
Mauna Kea, 18
Mauna Loa, 18
McKinley, 18
Mitchell, 13
Ozarks, 61, 107–108
Pacific Coast, 17–18
Rainier, 17
Rocky, 15–17
St. Helens, 29
Waialeale, 22
Whitney, 17
mud flows, 27
"must" to "want" settlement pattern, 60–61

NAFTA. *See* North American Free Trade Agreement
nation building, 74–76
Native Americans, 3, 32, 98
   Europe's impact on, 6, 36, 40, 49
native cultures, 32–35. *See also* Indians; indigenous cultures; Native Americans
   contributions of, 35, 37
   European impact on, 6, 36, 40, 49
   Hohokam, 33
   Inuit, 34–35, 40, 65–67
   on Pacific Coast, 34, 40
   physical characteristics of, 32
   Pueblo, 33, 40, 49
   religious conversion of, 49
   treaties and, 43
natural disasters, 26–29, 105, 106–107
natural environment, 83–84, 86
natural gas, 83, 89
natural hazards, 11
natural resources
   cultural history impacted by, 36–39
   diversity/abundance of, 1, 10–11, 31, 36, 83–84, 110
   frontier attitude toward, 6

impacts on/use of, 11
industry and, 86–90
migration and, 6
settlement and, 45
nature, gifts and challenges of, 10–29
New Amsterdam, 49. *See also* New York City
New England, 37–38, 95
Newfoundland, 35–36, 36, 49, 88, 95
New Mexico, 39, 49
New York City, 8, 52, 59, 95, 96, 103
New Zealand, 5
North America, 3, 94
North American Free Trade Agreement (NAFTA), 92
Northern America, 1–2, 3, 5. *See also* Canada; United States
   "Angloization" of, 40
   area/sq. miles of, 5, 6, 44
   European impacts on, 3, 5–6, 8, 31–32, 35–43, 65, 70–71, 95
   future of, 104–110
   as global power, 7
   land surface occupied by, 82
   physical characteristics of, 4, 5
   population of, 5
   regions of, 9, 94–103
   unifying characteristics of, 5–8
Nova Scotia, 38, 49, 74
Nunavut, 65–67, 75, 78

oceans, 10, 17, 54, 82
Ontario, 58, 97
Orient, route to, 36
Ottawa, 58, 59, 78, 95
overpopulation, 47, 82
owl, spotted, 78, 101

Pacific Coast, 22, 34, 40, 101–103
   mountains and valleys, 17–18
Pacific culture region, the, 5, 45
Pacific Northwest, 75, 78
Pacific ranges, 21
Pacific Ring of Fire, 28
parks, national, 79

INDEX

Parliament, 77
pension plans, 93
people. *See* humans
petroleum, 83, 89, 99, 109
the Piedmont, 13
Pilgrims, 39, 68
plains
    agriculture and soils on, 10, 14
    Atlantic and Gulf Coastal, 12–13
    Central, 14
    farming on, 12, 83
    Great, 14, 29, 99, 109
    Indians, 34
    in interior, 12
    interior lowland, 14
    western, 99–100
plantations, 39, 51, 89
plants, 20
plateaus, 12
    Colorado, 15
    Columbia, 15
    Fraser, 16
    interior, 15–17
plow, steel-tipped moldboard, 56
Plymouth, Massachusetts, 38, 39
polar regions, 10
political geography, 73–80
political stability, 78
politics, 43, 94, 108–109
pollution, water/air, 6, 23
popular culture, 7–8, 13, 59, 71–72, 102–103
populations, 5. *See also* minorities; overpopulation; *specific locations*
    aging, 47–48, 93
    declines in, 57, 61, 99, 107
    density, 44–46, 54
    growth of, 44–45, 47, 51, 55, 58–62, 107–109
    immigration and, 47, 107
    map, 46
    property values and, 29, 61
    settlement and, 44–62
    soils and, 12
    water and, 22, 54–55

Port Royal (Nova Scotia), 38
ports. *See* seaports
postal services, 74
precipitation, 20–22. *See also specific types*
presidents, 76, 77
prime ministers, 76, 77
Promontory Summit, 41
property values, 29, 61
Protestantism, 5, 68, 84
provinces, 62, 74–75, 78, 108, 109
public lands, 74, 78–79
Puget Sound region, Washington, 56
Puritans, 38, 68

Quebec, 59, 74, 84, 97
Quebec City, 38, 43, 55, 59, 97
Quebec, French, 65, 78, 109
Quebecois, 65

railroads, 41–42
    Chinese people and, 42, 51
    economy and, 83, 85
    government and, 80
    settlements and, 53–57
rain, 20, 22, 26
ranching, 88, 99. *See also* livestock
ranges
    Bitterroot, 15
    Brooks, 15
    Canadian Pacific, 21
    Cascade, 17, 21
    Coast, 17–18
    Columbia, 15
    Sangre de Cristo, 15
    Sierra Nevada, 17, 21, 40, 55
    tidal, 11
regions, 2–3, 94–103, 95. *See also specific regions*
    changes in, 109–110
    characteristics of, 3, 5
    culture, 1–9, 2–5, 63, 94
    eastern core, 95–98
    heartland, 98–101
    West Coast, 101–103

INDEX

religions, 5. *See also specific religions*
    Europe and, 67, 70
    freedom to worship and, 67–69
    Spain, natives and, 49
    symbols and, 63, 67–69
relocation diffusion, 51
reservoirs, 12, 23, 25
resources, 82. *See also specific resources*
    government, land and, 78–80
    humans as, 45, 48, 82, 110
retirement, 47, 61, 74, 93, 107
rivers, 10, 13, 23–25
    Amazon/Congo, 23
    Clark Fork, 15–16
    Colorado, 24–25, 26, 55, 105
    Columbia, 25, 55
    Hudson, 25, 49
    hydroelectric power and, 14
    Mackenzie, 25
    Mississippi, 23–24, 37, 54, 55, 89, 96
    Missouri, 23–24
    Ohio, 23–24, 55
    Rio Grande, 24, 105
    St. Lawrence, 14, 23, 25, 37–38, 54, 55, 97
    Tennessee, 25
    Willamette, 55
    Yukon, 25
roads, 57, 74. *See also* highways
Rocky Mountains, 15–17
Rostlund, Erhard, 104, 110
rural areas, 79, 107–108
rural-to-urban settlement pattern, 59
Russia, 40–41, 51, 75
Rustbelt, 60, 98

Salton Sea, 16
San Andreas Fault, 28
SARS (severe acute respiratory syndrome), 92
Saunders, Sir Charles, 42
scablands, 15
Scandinavian settlers, 38, 40, 51
seaports, 12–13, 54–55, 61, 96

Senate, 77, 96
separatism, 65–67
service-related activities, 90, 97, 98, 109
settlements, 20, 45
    agriculture, water and, 24–26, 56
    boom-and-bust cycle of, 57
    cities and, 57–62
    early, 48–49
    economic development and, 6, 10, 45, 62, 79
    Europe and, 31, 37–40, 48–51
    factors influencing, 57–58
    future of, 61–62
    in interior West, 17
    migration and, 50–53, 109–110
    natural resources and, 45
    patterns, 9, 58–61
    population and, 44–62
    railroads and, 53–57
    transportation and, 12–13, 53, 59, 61
Seward, William Henry, 75
shipping, 12, 23–24, 53, 54, 80
Sikhism, 69
silver, 37, 84, 99
skiing, 12, 83, 95, 100
skraelings, 35
slaves, 39, 50–51
snow, 26, 66
Snowbelt, 60
social equality, 5
social services, 74
society, 63, 63–72
socioeconomic mobility, 7
soils
    agriculture and, 10, 14, 42
    in Canadian shield, 14
    diversity of, 20
    erosion of, 6, 106
    fertility and farming, 55–56, 88
    laws protecting, 80
    population and, 12
South America, 3
South, U.S., 39, 51, 110

INDEX

Southwest, 10, 99, 105, 110
Spain, 37, 39, 49, 75, 79, 98
Spanish language, 67
St. Lawrence, Gulf of, 12, 36
St. Lawrence River, 14, 23, 25, 37–38, 54, 55, 97
St. Lawrence Seaway, 23
St. Lawrence Valley, 14, 40, 49, 95
storms, 26–28,
suburban areas, 59–60, 98
summers, 20
Sunbelt, 60, 83, 99
Supreme Court, 78
symbols, 63–69

taiga, 22, 34
tariffs, 91–92
taxes, 60, 80
technology, 54, 70–71, 85, 88, 90
temperatures, 20–22, 60, 105
Tennessee River Authority (TVA), 25
territorial expansion, 74–76
terrorism, 85
Thanksgiving, 8, 35
tidal ranges, 11
tornadoes, 26, 28, 105
Toronto, 59, 95–96
tourism
    development and, 17
    in eastern core, 95, 97
    economy and, 83, 92
    in heartland, 99–101
    landform type for, 12
    settlement and, 57, 58
towns, spacing of, 56–57
trade, 82, 87, 90–93, 99–100
trains. *See* railroads
transportation. *See also* automobiles; railroads; shipping
    linkages, 12–13, 17
    settlement and, 12–13, 53, 59, 61
    water for, 25–26, 40
travel, 2, 26, 41, 56–57, 71
treaties, 43
trees, 89, 106. *See also* logging

tsunamis, 26, 105
tundra, 22, 34
TVA. *See* Tennessee River Authority

unemployment, 92
United States (U.S.). *See also specific cities/regions/states*
    agriculture in, 42, 96–97
    area/sq. miles of, 44
    Canada border with, 52, 72
    cities in Canada and, 59–60, 95–103
    Civil War, 78
    culture of Canada v., 1–2, 8, 31
    debt/trade deficit of, 92–93
    eastern core of, 95–98
    flags of, 64, 96
    governments of Canada v., 60, 76–78, 108–109
    heartland region of, 98–101
    language, diversity and stability in, 67
    minorities in, 2, 61, 72, 103, 108
    national motto of, 6–7
    nation building and, 74–76
    politics and, 94, 108–109
    population of Canada v., 44–48
    relationship with other countries, 70
    South, 39, 51, 110
    taxes in Canada v., 60
    trade between Canada and, 91–92
    travel between Canada and, 2
    water, Canada and, 92, 105
    westward expansion and, 40–42, 51–53, 74–76
uranium, 83
urban areas. *See also* conurbation
    in eastern core, 97–98
    rural-to-, settlement patterns, 59
    to suburban settlement pattern, 59–60
    zoning in, 80
urbanization, 5, 12, 42
urban renewal, 62, 107

INDEX

valleys, 13
   Central, 17, 56, 102
   Death, 17, 21–22
   Fraser River, 56
   Imperial, 17
   Napa, 102
   Ohio, 40
   Pacific Coast, 17–18
   St. Lawrence, 14, 40, 49, 95
   Willamette, 17, 56, 102
values, 29, 61, 71, 108
vegetation, 20, 22
Verrazano, Giovanni da, 37
Victoria, Queen, 58
Vikings, 35–36
volcanoes, 15, 17–18, 26, 28–29, 105

wars, 42, 78
Washington, DC, 58, 95, 96
water, 10–11. *See also* floods; groundwater; lakes; oceans; rain; rivers
   attraction of, 54–55
   California and, 26, 55, 105
   Canada, U.S. and, 92, 105
   changes in, 104, 105, 110
   of eastern v. western Northern America, 23
   economic development and, 25–26
   as environmental hazard, 26–28
   features, 22–26
   human use of, 25–26
   laws protecting, 80
   place names and, 26, 54
   pollution, 6, 23
   population and, 22, 54–55
   saline, 16
   settlement, agriculture and, 24–26, 56
   for transportation, 25–26, 40
   for travel, 26, 41
weather, 18. *See also* climates
West Coast region, 101–103
Western Hemisphere, 2–3
westward expansion, 31, 40–42, 51–53, 56
wilderness areas, 79
wildlife, 22, 34, 83. *See also* animals
winds, 21
wineries, 102
winters, 20
woodlands, 20, 29, 33–34, 40, 89, 105

PICTURE CREDITS

page:

4:	© Mapping Specialists, Ltd.	58:	© New Millennium Images
8:	© KRT/NMI	66:	© Reuters Photo Archive/NMI
16:	© New Millennium Images	68:	© AFP/NMI
19:	© Mapping Specialists, Ltd.	77:	© Zuma Press/NMI
21:	© Layne Kennedy/CORBIS	84:	© KRT/NMI
24:	© New Millennium Images	87:	© Mapping Specialists, Ltd.
27:	© Reuters Photo Archive/NMI	91:	© KRT/NMI
33:	© New Millennium Images	96:	© New Millennium Images
38:	© New Millennium Images	100:	© KRT/NMI
41:	© National Archives of Canada/NMI	102:	© New Millennium Images
46:	© Mapping Specialists, Ltd.	106:	© Matthew Mcvay/CORBIS
50:	© KRT/NMI	Cover:	© James P. Blair/CORBIS
52:	© New Millennium Images		

ABOUT THE CONTRIBUTORS

KRISTI L. DESAULNIERS is an educator who enjoys incorporating her international teaching experiences with students' learning. As an elementary school teacher with a master's degree in geography, Desaulniers has taught in England, Switzerland, and her home state of South Dakota. She studied as a Keizai Koho Center Fellow in Japan and was the recipient of a Distinguished Teaching Achievement Award from the National Council for Geographic Education. She also taught in Canada on a Fulbright exchange, where she had the opportunity to explore much of the beautiful landscape described in *Northern America*. Her love of learning about people and places has taken her to many locations around the globe. Currently, she resides in Sioux Falls, South Dakota, with her husband, Rob, and their children, Dawson and Aida.

CHARLES F. "FRITZ" GRITZNER is Distinguished Professor of Geography at South Dakota State University in Brookings. He is now in his fifth decade of college teaching, scholarly research, and writing. In addition to teaching, he enjoys traveling, writing, working with teachers, and sharing his love of geography with students and readers alike. As the consulting editor and frequent author for the Chelsea House MODERN WORLD NATIONS and MODERN WORLD CULTURES series, he has a wonderful opportunity to combine each of these "hobbies." Gritzner has traveled extensively in all 50 states (including having lived in 7) and throughout much of Canada.

Professionally, Gritzner has served as both president and executive director of the National Council for Geographic Education (NCGE). He has received numerous awards in recognition of his academic and teaching achievements, including the NCGE's George J. Miller Award for Distinguished Service to geography and geographic education.